MW01593482

Fields

of

Grace

2 CO: 12: 9

Billy Shoffner

Endorsements for Fields of Grace

I have known Billy Shoffner for over thirty years as a fellow Pastor, a proven man of God, and as a true friend that you can always look to. We have ministered together in different types of services such as retreats, ordination services, and exchange of pulpits. We have traveled and ministered together in Africa where our hearts were stirred for World Missions. When others thought he was ready to retire, he gave himself to work in Nicaragua, Central America, planting and building churches. After reading his first book, *Fields of Grace*, I know him even better.

—James Walker

Founder/Director, Outreach Christian Fellowship

A Helping Hand to Missionaries

The influence of the powerful phenomenon we call Grace is probably without equal. Indeed, such influence cannot be found elsewhere. For more than fifty years, Billy Shoffner has influenced my life toward good as missionary pastor, mentor, counselor, and friend. In this account, the reader is drawn into the narrative of a common man taken captive by a most uncommon Master. Affectionately known as Brother Billy by acquaintances Christian and non-Christian alike, his story evokes wonder, pleasure, and a sweet magnetism stirring us to enter our own equally verdant fields of grace.

—Jerry Lout

Global Outreach mobilizer-mentor

Founder International Community Outreach

Amazing Grace. A man of grace. A ministry of grace. Billy Shoffner has been a spiritual father to me for over twenty years. In that time, I have seen God work in him and through him in so many significant ways. The pages of this book are from his heart after more than fifty years of faithful life and ministry. This is more than a memoir. It is a testimony to God's faithfulness and how God's grace will flow when men and women humbly submit themselves to the call and will of God and commit themselves to building the Kingdom of His Son, Jesus Christ.

—Aaron Bequette
Senior Pastor
Northside Christian Center Carthage, Texas

Fields of Grace by Brother Billy Shoffner is an account of the sixty-year ministry of a true man of God. In it he reveals a tale of life's adventures, ministerial trials, and the miracles of God. He allows us a glimpse into is pastor's family life. He further lays out all what the churches experienced during his tenure and what happened at the mission churches he helped build. After reading the account of his walk of faith, I am encouraged in my own faith and, in some degree, ashamed of my lack of faith. Thank you, Brother Billy, for your honesty and openness in sharing your life's work.

—John W. Boland
Author of Workplace Evangelism:
Taking Your Faith to Work
Principal, Northside Christian Academy
President, Mission Carthage

Fields
of
Grace

Billy Shoffner

TATE PUBLISHING
AND ENTERPRISES, LLC

Fields of Grace
Copyright © 2015 by Billy Shoffner. All rights reserved.

No part of this publication may be reproduced, stored in a retrieval system or transmitted in any way by any means, electronic, mechanical, photocopy, recording or otherwise without the prior permission of the author except as provided by USA copyright law.

This book is designed to provide accurate and authoritative information with regard to the subject matter covered. This information is given with the understanding that neither the author nor Tate Publishing, LLC is engaged in rendering legal, professional advice. Since the details of your situation are fact dependent, you should additionally seek the services of a competent professional.

The opinions expressed by the author are not necessarily those of Tate Publishing, LLC.

Published by Tate Publishing & Enterprises, LLC
127 E. Trade Center Terrace | Mustang, Oklahoma 73064 USA
1.888.361.9473 | www.tatepublishing.com

Tate Publishing is committed to excellence in the publishing industry. The company reflects the philosophy established by the founders, based on Psalm 68:11,
"The Lord gave the word and great was the company of those who published it."

Book design copyright © 2015 by Tate Publishing, LLC. All rights reserved.
Cover design by Joseph Emnace
Interior design by Manolito Bastasa

Published in the United States of America

ISBN: 978-1-63418-068-9
Religion / Christian Ministry / Missions
14.11.18

This book is dedicated to the many, many friends and church members whom I have known over the years, whose lives make up the material written in this manuscript. To the many pastors and teachers who have so faithfully ministered and taught me so many things concerning ministry, dedication goes out to my present pastor, Aaron Bequette, who has helped me in so many areas of ministry that I had missed along the way, but I give honor and glory to God above all for bringing to memory so many of the experiences and events written here.

Fields of Grace is dedicated to my wife, Betty Shoffner, and family who have stood by me faithfully and gave me their support of confidence that I needed while writing, also to friends who encouraged me to write.

Acknowledgments

I want to thank Tate Publishing for the encouragement they shared with me to continue writing my book on grace. They have been inspiring along the way, and without their encouragement I may have become discouraged and never completed the book. Thanks, Tate Publishing, for standing with me.

I offer thanks to the Lord for giving me inspiration to write this book, which I had wrestled with for months.

I am very grateful to my family for supporting my work on this book, and especially my wife for the confidence she placed in me for writing.

Third and last but not least, gratitude is given to Mrs. Kacy Edgmon for the many hours she spent in editing and helping prepare the manuscript for printing. I am pretty excited to know we are getting closer to printing. Thanks again, Kacy, for the work you have spent. Love you and your family.

I wish to express my thanks to Mrs. Cathe Temmerman and to Mrs. Peggy Thorthon for their work on working through the edits of my book to prepare it for print.

Contents

Introduction

The purposed intention for this book is to share with our many friends and those we have pastored over the many years of ministry the many events and experiences that time and space did not allow us to communicate. We trust that within the pages of this manuscript, you will find some depth of God's love, which will disclose the desire for a relationship, which every God-called pastor longs to have. A relationship structured by caring and praying for his flock, rejoicing with them, weeping with them, and just sharing a meal with the family. Also to get a glimpse of a church family that is not controlled by a religious system and that has to depend on an organization to sustain them but is rather a church body that has to lean heavily upon prayer and faith to maintain their ministry needs.

Hopefully you might understand that God does have a plan that does not have to depend completely upon the wealth of another to survive. The strength of family is also disclosed in this book and that the family is designed by God to structure strength and power of the church body. We give thanks to our Father God for giving us inspiration in His Spirit to write. We trust you will enjoy the thoughts and love that has gone into the words of this book.

An Unfolding of His Grace

It Started With a Miracle

(Ps. 139:7–10, KJV) Raised on an East Texas farm, I had never gotten any farther from the house than thirty miles before reaching the age of eighteen, so you can see I was raised within a very small world. When your world is as small as mine, you have plenty to learn about the world that lies out there before your journey in life really begins.

I was raised to love school and church and was raised in a semi-Christian home. I say semi because while Mother was a wonderful Christian lady, Dad never embraced church life. Therefore, Dad was never exposed to the Gospel, so he didn't think he really needed Jesus to be in his life. Mother and us kids went to church when we had the opportunity but lived quite a distance from the church, so we could not go every Sunday. At a very early age, I was convinced of my sin, had received the Lord Jesus as my savior, had attended church when possible, and also attended the gospel singing that we would have around in Red River County.

Wandered Away from the Fold

At the age of seventeen, I graduated from high school in the year of 1947 at Bogota High School and did not make an effort to attend any higher education. Since there were no jobs available, I went to Dallas to find work and to live there with my cousin. I worked for a seat-covering factory for a few months. I grew tired of the job and went to work for a photograph company that went house to house taking pictures of babies and young children.

At this time of my life, I became careless with my relationship with the Lord and let my job interfere with attending church, and before I knew what was happening, I began to wander away from the Lord and away from my church. I took up drinking and soon discovered that I was an alcoholic and could not really concentrate on my work without having something to drink. I was drifting away from God, losing my perspective of a Christian life and also withdrawing from those who loved me and tried to help direct me back to Christ and His grace. I was like a sheep wandering away from its shepherd and walking farther away from the Shepherd's voice. It seemed that nothing could turn me around, so I kept falling deeper and deeper into the pits of the world and its control.

Called Out of Darkness

God's grace does not work because we are righteous or that we are doing good things but because He loves us wherever and whatever we are doing. Even though I had drifted so far from the Shepherd's will, I could still hear that small still voice in the night when I would lie down to sleep. When I would go to my room so intoxicated that it was difficult to lie on my bed for it seemed that I was lying upon the waves of the sea that tossed me up and down, I would never fail to pray in my heart because it seemed that Jesus was always there. I am not recommending that anyone should ever tempt God in such a way as this, but what I am saying is God loves us so much that even when we try to run away from Him, He is there because we never reach a place in life that God can't reach us.

It Started With a Miracle

> (Psalms 139:7–10, NKJV) Where can I go from Your Spirit? Or where can I flee from Your presence? **8** If I ascend into heaven, You *are* there; If I make my bed in hell, behold, You *are there*. **9** *If* I take the wings of the morning, *And* dwell in the uttermost parts of the sea, **10** Even there Your hand shall lead me, And Your right hand shall hold me. I had reached a place in my life where everything was growing darker and darker, but God in His mercy and grace called me out of darkness into His marvelous light!

In 1949, while working with this photography company in Atlanta, Georgia, suddenly, on the spur of the moment, I was stopped in my tracks one night around 11:00 p.m. I was out drinking and carousing with buddies when, very plainly, I heard in my heart, "Go home!" At first, I tried to shut out the voice and ignore its message, but it would not go away. It seemed to become a controlling voice that was commanding me to go home. This is when Jesus called me in the night and called me out of darkness and into His marvelous light. I took a cab as quickly as possible and rushed back to my room.

I was working as a team at that time with a young man from Erie, Pennsylvania. When I reached my room, I immediately awoke Hank, the man I worked with, and said, "Hank, I am going home." He rose up in bed and said, "Are you crazy? What are you talking about?" He really thought I was drunk and talking out of my head, but I finally made him understand that I am out of here as soon as possible. We called the bus station to find out when the next bus was leaving going toward Texas. They informed us there was one leaving at midnight.

I threw my clothes and other belongings into a suitcase, and a few minutes before midnight, I had my ticket and was on board. I was headed home to family and friends, not really knowing what would transpire when I reached home; but right then, that was a minor problem. I found out that my real problem was finding my way back to my place in Christ and in the church. Everyone was so happy to see me and have me back home, but I knew very well that within me there was some real reconciling to be done, both with God and with man. I was not real sure just how that was going to play out, but I placed myself on trial until I had gotten my life in line with God's will.

To you who have strayed away from your first love and drifted back into sin, please don't get discouraged and give up the battle thinking it will be just like it was before going astray; you may have to press in for a while before finding your place once again. Please don't quit and look back when you don't feel anything or feel high emotions, because we don't come into God by feelings and emotions but by sheer faith in Jesus: He is there, that is His name; stretch and touch him with your faith. He loves you, and after the test, you will receive the joy!

I found this to be true in my life, and this joy is the real thing and never leaves you, so receive it by faith. I know, because this joy I have has remained for almost sixty years and has grown to be my constant companion; while others doubt and fear, it will rise up and shout in the ear of the wicked one to let him know that what you have received from your God is the real thing! "For the joy of the Lord is your strength" (Nehemiah 8:10B, KJV).

In 1954, I suppose you could call me one of those good old boys who never broke the law and always looked good in the eyes of the public. They say you don't know the contents of a book until you open the covers and look inside. Well, no one knew the contents of this book like God, and when He began to read and expose the story, everyone knew. This is exactly what happened to this old country boy. I had lived the last few years of my life in total debauchery—drinking, smoking, and trying to fulfill the lust of the flesh. Needless to say, this road is short, ends quickly, and leaves its possessor lying by the wayside half-dead.

I am sure you are well acquainted with the story of the Good Samaritan as he found his victim lying by the roadside half dead. Understand when a person is dead spiritually he is half dead, and that was my case. I had allowed my relationship with the Lord to wane away until I had no spiritual life left in me. I was that victim lying beside the road side, just waiting.

Where man's strength and ability comes to an end is where God's love and grace begins. I found myself slowly but surely dying with a stomach condition. Anything I ate within thirty minutes put me into pains and cramps that I could no longer bear.

This is where the miracle begins. Our family was raised in Baptist doctrine and didn't know there was any other way, so whatever a person is taught, that's what he becomes and usually stays the rest of his life. Let's set the record straight up front: we are not being critical of our Baptist Churches or of our Baptist friends. I love the Baptists; in fact, I have just resigned from a missionary Baptist Church where I served thirteen years and loved every day of it. I received my foundation from the Baptists; we are not writing to divide churches but are here to unify the Lord's people wherever they serve. I just simply found something that led me into a brand-new experience with the Lord Jesus—an experience that I have found to have made the promises of God come alive in my life. Promises that I once looked at wishing they could be real to me but could never seem to get my hands on them until the Holy Spirit filled me. Along with the infilling of the Holy Spirit came a faith that I had never known before; it came alive and the promises that I only hoped for seem to become substance and evidence of things I had hoped for. A new field of grace had just begun to seed and break through the darkness of the earth that had held its life in captivity. Now the darkness that I had groped in vanished, and light broke through, the marvelous light that put a song of praise in my heart and a new day had dawned that brought me into a greater relationship with Jesus Christ my Savior. Well, all of this changed the religious perspective in the life of my immediate family.

There was a little woman by the name of Nora Noah who came into our community of Marro to hold a revival. She wasn't a Baptist; she was one of them who spoke in tongues, believed God still healed people of diseases, and believed the gifts of the Holy Spirit are still available to those who believe. That didn't fit anything I had heard my preacher say, so I stayed as far away from it as possible. My mamma didn't; she received it with all her heart and brought it home with her to all of us. Well, the Spirit is kind of contagious, and I guess I hadn't received my vaccination so that it got a hold of me. Let me tell you why. Remember I mentioned I had a health issue that was taking me away from this world? This message of the Holy Spirit was offering me life and healing, and I felt like I needed to live a bit longer.

On a Wednesday night, when my mother came home from her prayer service, she noticed I was up and walking around, walking around because I was in so much pain that I couldn't sleep. As she came into my room, she asked, "Billy, would you like for me to pray for you?" And that night, I found out that what I had been so fearful of was the very thing that would prolong my life. I answered with a doubtful voice, "I guess so, anything now."

The first miracle came as Mother laid her hand on me and began to pray a simple prayer like this: "Jesus, you are the same Jesus as you were when you were here walking the shores of Galilee and the streets of Jerusalem healing the sick. Now, Father, heal Billy. I pray in the name of Jesus."

The miracle was glorious and wonderful; I felt it as warm oil was poured out over my body, and the pain left. I slept well through the night, got up the next morning early as I had to travel sixty miles to work, ate a big breakfast, and went off to work. I was feeling kind of strange since I was feeling no pain after eating breakfast, and that whole day, I felt no pain. What I am about to write shames me deeply. I was so full of rebelling that I would not tell my mother about my healing because I didn't want her to get the joy out of thinking her prayer brought healing to me, what a shame. From Wednesday until Saturday morning, I remained silent about my healing. You see I still had this thing about religion. Religion, what a dreadful thing to create such an attitude. But when Saturday morning arrived and Mother came into the room where I was sitting, I could hold it back no longer. She never asked, but I was compelled to say, "Mother, I will not have to go see the doctor today. I am healed." Joy kicked in about this time, and Mother did a little dance right there in our living room. I will never forget that wonderful day. What a God of grace we serve, one who will bless a person who is as stubborn as I.

This was the beginning of my journey with Jesus. God, if it is all as good as this, I am in it for the long haul. Well, sixty years of serving a gracious and loving God have expired, and the end ain't yet.

He Is the Real Thing

I got smart enough to figure out that if God is good enough to heal a stubborn person as me, then I should trust Him with all my life and serve Him. Immediately, I started worshiping in the church my mother went to and became so hungry for the Holy Spirit that each night, at the end of the message when the invitation was given, I made my way to the altar and stayed there until everyone became tired and had to go home. This procedure went on for around three months, and I still had not received the baptism of the Spirit, but I didn't give up. I was convinced that God's Word said this gift was for everyone who would believe would receive, so I went right on visiting the altars each evening until He came.

When He came, it was in a very quiet and soft way. We were having an outside revival; Sister Nora Noah was the evangelist. At the end of her message, as usual, I went to the altar to pray and wait upon the Lord. I was sitting flat on the ground when one of the men who had come with Sister Noah walked by me and said, "Billy, do you think you will receive the Holy Spirit?"

"Yes," I answered.

"Do you think you will receive Him right now?"

This question startled me because each night, when I prayed and waited to receive the Holy Spirit, my thoughts were that I am going to be filled, but not just now; it will be at another time. To his last question, I answered, "I do," and when I said I do, He did. The Holy Spirit came in a measure that I had never experienced before or after. He is the real thing because when He made His entrance into my life, He began to speak in a language I had never heard before. He continued to speak in this heavenly language until it suddenly dawned upon me that the Holy Spirit had come and filled and baptized me in His wonderful life, the life of the Lord Jesus Christ. A new day dawned into my life, and I have never been the same since that wonderful hour.

After the Holy Spirit filled me, I began to discover the changes in my life. I had been an alcoholic; the desire to drink was gone forever. I had been a chain smoker, at least two packs a day, and I had no more desire for nicotine; the lust of the flesh had been overcome. I discovered I had become a "new creation in Christ Jesus," and the joy came with all of this. I can now say He is the real thing!

One Giant Step

You know God has strange ways to get us to a certain place and have us meet a certain person. As time went by, I continued to serve God in revivals around our area. One evening, I was supposed to meet my girlfriend at a revival service at Cut Hand, Texas. When I arrived, my girlfriend was with another girl by the name of Betty Williams, and until this day, I still don't know just how God arranged this. When the meeting was over, I took my girlfriend and Betty to Betty's house; I wound up walking Betty to the door and asking if I could see her the next evening. She gave a positive answer. Wow! God doesn't lose time. Well, at this time of my life at twenty-four years of age, time was an important issue, and God knew that better than me or Betty.

In the time of our short engagement, many humorous things took place. To name a few, the day I bought her engagement ring, I had a wreck and totaled my car, and when I went to give it to her, I laughingly said, "God might have been trying to tell me something important," but she still loved me anyway. When we were dating, I had a car that was using a quart of oil about every fifty miles, so as we were going to church, the smoke filled the car so bad we could hardly see each other or barely breathe. I felt fortunate to get Betty home and back to my home that night. We were married in June 1954 by a country preacher by the name of Lewis Clark. June 12, 2014 marked sixty years of a happy marriage that has been fruitful and profitable for the kingdom of God. To us has been born three of the greatest children we could have ever asked for: Michael Lynn, Rebecca Ann, and, last but not least, David Glenn. We are thankful for three great children who have made a difference in the lives of many people.

The Miracles Continue

The year 1954 was a year that filled up our lives with new and blessed things. On June 12, Betty and I made our covenant of marriage with each other; I was saved and filled with the Holy Spirit and received a miracle of healing. I received my call into the ministry of preaching God's Word; we were moved out into the ministry field before any formal Bible schooling or teaching. We went out by faith in the call of ministry. To make full explanation of our ministry, I must share the manner of how the Lord called me.

It happened this way: Sunday afternoon before I made my surrender to preach before the church that night, I was praying alone. As I prayed, the Holy Spirit spoke and said, "Go into the highways and hedges with your feet shod with the preparation of the gospel of peace, and compel my people to come into my house, that my house may be full." With that confirmation and assurance, I submitted my commitment before the Lord and the church I was attending at the time. When I made my announcement, the Holy Spirit fell upon the church, and the people present were ministered to in wonderful ways. My wife was slain in the Spirit and received some glorious scenes of heaven and people whom she knew were there. This was the second step of our journey in ministry.

The Doors Begin to Open

From the world's perspective, I was not prepared to start preaching, had no formal training in Bible school, and had not very much study of the Word, but ready or not, the doors began to open. We began to walk through them, taking every opportunity possible to preach the Gospel of Christ. The questions remain: How much training does it take? How much Bible school must you have to declare the Word of God? Until this day, that question has not been answered with my understanding because we are finishing up fifty-nine years of pastoring, evangelizing, and missionary ministering and have gone forward only with the call, the anointing, and the assurance of God with confirmation of the fruit that comes from preaching the Gospel of Christ.

My First Message

Everyone was set on me preaching there at the little church we attended at the time, so ready or not, I make my first appearing and message. A friend of mine, Mildred Roach, and I had moved an old store building onto the lot that my dad had given to the church. When unloading the building, we had placed it upon wood blocks about two feet long, so the building's foundation was made of two-feet-long wood blocks. When the night of my first message had arrived, there had been a bad windstorm that day, so when we got to the church, we immediately knew we had a big problem. If I remember correctly, the west side of the church was on the ground and the east side was still elevated on the blocks.

I suppose normal people would have dismissed the service and gone back home, but not this group. We marched right in, took our seats as if nothing had happened, sang, and preached. I preached my first message in a building that had been blown off its foundation. To say the least, this was an unusual situation. My first sermon was "When God Delivered His People from Egypt." Strange as it may seem, I remember it as clear today as I did that stormy night with one side of the church sitting on the ground. I was in another world as I declared how the power of God wrought the mighty miracles of judgment against Egypt and how Israel ate the first Passover Supper that delivered them from the iron furnace of the Egyptians by the precious blood of the Lamb that had been placed on the doorpost and lentils of Israel's homes. How God's people walked out of there at midnight without even a dog wagging his tongue against them, and when they arrived at the Red Sea in our message, the preacher stopped preaching, got happy, and had to shout a little bit. This was the first of many, many messages and teachings over the years of ministering God's Word.

Our First Pastor Experience

Glad Tidings Tabernacle was our very first church to pastor, located in Mount Pleasant, Texas. Glad Tidings Tabernacle was built and directed by a well-known minister of the forties and fifties by the name of GM. He has been named the man who prayed for OR when he was healed of stuttering and tuberculosis. We were copastoring for him. The church was very small in number, but the people we had were very warm, friendly, and loved Jesus, so that was enough. We were following the cloud, trying to stay up with what the Lord chose for us to do, but the way was very narrow. However, we didn't realize it because the grace of God was so wonderfully blessing us with the kind of blessings that men can't give.

Betty was carrying our first child at the time, and we were receiving a very small amount of money from the church. Sister Myrtle M. was letting us live in part of her house. Now, when Betty and I think of the little apartment in Myrtle's house, we laugh and still wonder how we did it. The apartment had only one room, a kitchen and bedroom combined. We used Sister Myrtle's sitting room when someone came to see us. Betty's due date came, and we had no money for her to get into the hospital. I was selling family Bibles at the time, so that morning, I prayed hard and asked God to lead me to someone who needed Bibles, and He wonderfully answered my prayer. I must boast on the Lord's grace for helping me because of any stretch of the imagination, I was no salesman, I was a preacher.

That Saturday morning, God gave me favor with almost every person I visited; I sold five big family Bibles that brought me twenty-five dollars, just enough to admit Betty into the hospital for her delivery. She birthed a beautiful baby boy, whom we named Michael Lynn. We named him after the angel Michael, the strong one who watches over God's people of Israel. Michael is now fifty-eight years old, and he has remained strong in his faith in God and is serving God faithfully. He is a man who loves people and will go the second mile to help those who are in need.

We brought Michael home the next day, and somehow, he got his nights and days all mixed up. When he wanted to sleep, we needed to work; when he wanted to remain awake, he demanded everyone's attention and got it. He had a great set of lungs, and he used them for days, until he finally figured out that he would join the party and sleep while everyone else was sleeping.

We remained at Glad Tidings Tabernacle for about one year and witnessed God's love and grace as we worked with the people. Our congregation was very small, consisting of around thirty people, but people we loved and who loved us. One rainy day, when I couldn't get outside to work, I had lain down across the bed when I heard a knock at the door. I arose to answer it, and a man stood there in the doorway and said, "The Lord sent me here to give you this." He placed a one-hundred-dollar bill in my hand. I did not know the man and wondered how he knew me, but to my knowledge, this was another miracle of God's grace, and this deserved our deepest praise and thanksgiving. At the time this man came and ministered help to us, we had no money. How wonderful it is to live by faith and see God's hand of mercy stretched out, offering us His love.

A Poor Rich Church

One day, as we went about our work around the church, we received a call from a little town out in West Texas by the name of Wellington. We had never been there but knew a family who lived there. Ethel Williams was the one who was calling, and when I answered, the voice on the other end said, "Will you come to Wellington and preach a revival for us?" Without giving it much thought and having no prayer about the matter, I answered, "Yes, I will come." Somewhere in my heart, I felt a tug to go to Wellington at this time in reply to the call. We set a date, and soon, I was on a Trailways bus, headed to who knows where. But one thing I knew in my heart was that I was an excited young preacher less than two years into ministry, and someone calls me to come and preach a revival. This call changed the course of my ministry forever because of the rich experiences I received in that poor little rich church.

When I arrived in Wellington, I found the people there were very disturbed because of a tornado that had just recently come through and devastated part of the town. It took out the east side of the city, not touching the west side, so being the man of faith and knowledge that I was, I figured this was the perfect situation for a revival to start. The people are anxious and upset because of the recent storm, so that will make it easy to reach them with the Gospel. Well, not 100 percent right, but certainly not 100 percent wrong because we had a Holy Ghost–filled revival in that city. People were revived, saved, and filled with the Spirit, and the little church rejoiced in each service.

A False Alarm

Sometimes things beyond our ability happen, and we just can't do one thing about it. I was staying with relatives, Jim and Ethel Williams. Jim was the fire chief for the city and lived upstairs at the fire station. This was Saturday night, and when we came in from the revival, everyone went to bed except me. I was still wound up tight over the revival service, so I wasn't ready to retire and was sitting up, reading and thinking about tomorrow's service. When I got ready to go to bed, I began looking for the light switch to turn off the lights; Ethel had done her ironing that day and had hung some of the clothes over the light switch, so the only switch I could see in the room was one that I thought was a little high on the wall and was red. I thought, *Oh well, this is a fire station and has red switches*, so I reached up to turn the lights off. This was not a good idea. In fact, this was my first big mistake that I made in Wellington, Texas. I am a country boy and not used to so many light switches.

Now you have got to see this. Two little grandsons who were acting like they were asleep on a pallet on the floor were not sleeping at all; they were watching me as I reached up to switch off the light. They knew full well what the switch was for; I flipped off the switch. Immediately, the fire alarm activated, and the sound began going off. There were about three things that happened in the next five minutes: first, the two boys who were supposed to be sleeping there on the floor were up on their feet, jumping, yelling, and laughing; Jim, the fire chief who was sleeping in the other room, jumped across the bed, hit the floor running to get to the alarm switch to turn it off. But no, I had flipped it off and set it to where it had to go the full time before it could be turned off.

Needless to say, the fire chief was very unhappy, but that is not the worst of the story. Remember, the town had just had a tornado that had ripped through the town, destroying much property; well, the townspeople thought the fire alarm was warning them that another tornado was on the way, so many of them jumped out of bed in their night clothes, frantic with fear. Remember now, it was midnight, and everyone was supposed to be asleep, but the alarm woke them. They jumped out of bed and hit the street running to the storm shelter; on second notice, when the people slowed down and observed, there were no clouds, no wind, and no sign of a storm. The moon was shining, but yours truly had awoken the town with a false alarm!

I was almost afraid to go out in public the next day, afraid someone would kill me, but the people there were very loving and forgiving so that I came through without a scratch. You remember it was mentioned earlier that this church experience changed the course of my life and ministry. It happened that I had been called to minister to a people who knew more of God's Word than I had ever heard, so this challenged me to be responsible to dig and study the Bible as never before. I had to feed someone who had much more knowledge than me. Well, I was young and I could pray, so I believed the Lord would help me obtain enough ability in the Word of God so that I could feed the people. I had forgotten it was not about me, but it was about Him who had called and sent me out. I turned to Him to give to me the revelation knowledge that would grow a church, and there at that little poor rich church, it happened.

You are pondering why I keep calling it a poor rich church. Well, this is why: it was very poor in materials and money. It was a little farming community that only had money during harvesttime; the people were very casual and dressed accordingly, but oh, how rich they were in the grace and love and knowledge of our Lord and Savior Jesus Christ. When we would begin to start a service, the Holy Spirit would come in His own sweet and graceful way to direct our worship and praise toward Jesus, and people would begin to respond to the gifts and callings that God had entrusted them with to bless and encourage others. It was like heaven on earth, and when the service was over, we could all witness that we had had a personal encounter with the Holy Spirit.

I found that within this environment one could grow quickly because the teacher, the instructor, the Holy Spirit was in charge, and Jesus said when He comes, He will teach you all things and He will glorify me. I witnessed the moving of the Holy Spirit as never before, and the riches of His Spirit and grace outweighed the poverty that no one ever seemed to notice, so now you know why you can be poor and rich all at the same time.

When our revival ended, I returned back to our home in Mount Pleasant, but I knew on my return home that God had already captured my heart for Wellington and made it one with the people at the little church there. The name of this church was Full Gospel Church, and it seemed to be the goal of the ministry there was to reach out and receive the fullness of the Gospel of Christ. Only a short time back at Glad Tidings Tabernacle at Mount Pleasant, I received another call from Wellington, and when I received the call, it was no surprise because the purpose of the call was "Will you come to Wellington and be our pastor?" Even now, my heart fills up as I remember the joy received from that call. I gladly answered without hesitation, "Yes, I will come, and when can you receive us?"

They said, "Come on when you are ready."

The Move to the West

At this time, we were driving a 1947 Dyno-Flo Dodge; it was a pretty dependable piece of transportation but had some miles and years on it. We hooked it up to a little two-wheel trailer and packed all our belongings—which consisted of a table, chairs, a bed, and refrigerator— in it and put our clothes in the backseat and trunk of the car. We said good-bye to the people at Glad Tidings Tabernacle and were on our way to the western part of Texas. It was Sunday evening, so we stopped at Faith Temple Church, the little church that we first attended, and attended the evening service there with the people whom we had first worshiped and served with. At the end of the service, we said our good-byes to our immediate family who attended there and to our friends. We set out for our new adventure of ministry to what seemed to us a far country.

Michael, our firstborn child, was six months old at that time. Looking back still causes chills and bumps to run up and down my back. This is the picture I still see in my mind: traveling six hundred miles at night in a car that is questionable of making a trip of that distance, a two-wheel trailer loaded with all the contents we owned in this world, a six-month-old baby, and not at all sure what we would encounter when we reached our destination. Also, our funds were really low, and we didn't know when or how they would be replenished. I can truly say we were moving on faith in God and the call to minister. God's wonderful grace has never failed nor forsaken us or our needs in all these fifty-nine years of ministry.

All of the above leaves our parents and church friends very concerned and anxious about how my family and I will survive the obstacles that we might encounter on the way.

After driving through mile after mile of darkness, we arrived at our destination as the sun rose up over the many acres of green cotton plants and the little city of Wellington. We were greeted there by my second cousin Ethel Williams, whom I have previously mentioned and whose husband is fire chief of the city. She invited us to live with them until we had secured a house for us to live in.

At this time, Betty and I felt much like Abram and Sarai must have felt when they left their homeland and family and journeyed to a land where they had no permanent dwelling place. But we were excited, following the Holy Spirit, believing that the God we served would be responsible for taking care of us, and He did. It was with joy. Our home for a while was an apartment owned by a man named Troy Garner; he was a well-to-do man. He loved the Lord and the church and became attached to us and the ministry we preached. He lowered the rent so that the church could handle it and our family could live comfortably for a while.

Excitement Starts in the House of the Lord

The poor little rich church was no exception to any other church; it had its problems and also its blessings. One thing I learned at Wellington Full Gospel was a principle that will never be forgotten: in the Lord's work, there is first a promise then a problem and then a provision. Every person that steps out on faith to serve the Lord must learn this principle. He can learn it the hard way, or he can make it easier on himself. If he is aware that it is a spiritual principle and flow with the system of the principle, it can come easier. But if he thinks he can improve upon the principles of God, he has a rude awakening, and it will still happen—promise, problem, and provision. Take it from the writer:

the provision is worth overcoming whatever problem that you may encounter getting through the problem.

This principle comes from the wilderness journeys of Israel. God gave them a promise of a land that flowed with milk and honey, and they embraced the thought of receiving those kinds of blessings, but they didn't realize that they would face a howling waste, barren desert to arrive at that promise. They did. Like many of us, they circled the same mountain for forty years before they were ready and prepared to overcome the problem and go into the Promised Land. The promise was there all the time, but they lived in the problem for forty years. Now, if we embrace and believe God's Word, we can shorten that time element, but if we choose to stay in the problem of the wilderness life, we may find ourselves buried in the wilderness.

Deuteronomy 30:19 (MSG) says, "I call Heaven and Earth to witness against you today: I place before you Life and Death, Blessing and Curse. Choose life so that you and your children will live." The Word says, "Choose you this day." Maybe the church has prolonged receiving the promises of God by hanging out in the wilderness life too long, and some of us even want to go back into Egypt so that we can feast on the flesh, garlic, and cucumbers, and dig out a living by watering the land artificially when all the time we could be eating from a land of promise, the land which is watered by the early and latter rains of God and where God becomes our strength and our health.

At the church at Wellington, the Holy Spirit flowed deep and wide and into the revelations of God's grace and love. We grew fast in the environment of the Holy Spirit and had its freedom to move upon the members of the church. The gifts of the Spirit would be activated many times in the services where people would stand and give out a prophetic message, and someone would be touched by the Holy Spirit and come to the altar to repent and receive Christ. At other times, someone would be given a song in the Spirit and begin to sing in the Spirit, making melody in their hearts to the Lord, and there was freedom in the spirit for me to stand and deliver a strong, anointed sermon to the people. Revival began shortly after we started our ministry at Full Gospel and continued until the day we decided to leave.

An Unexpected Revival

On a usual Sunday-evening meeting, we began to gather for church. All the people had gathered to begin worship. You must understand now that this was a farming area, and most of our people were farmers and lived quite a distance from the church. In the church, we had two families related to each other as grandparents, and their families consisted of Mom, Dad, and three children. One of those children was a very young boy, around three years old.

It happened that Sunday the family with the little boy visited Grandpa and Grandma and had eaten lunch with them, and then the mom, dad, and two oldest children had gone home and had left Little Eddie with his grandparents. Eddie's parents left for church, thinking the grandparents would bring him when they came to church. The grandparents, not knowing that Eddie had fallen asleep on the bed, thought that he was with his parents. To everyone's surprise, the grandparents had not thought to pick Little Eddie up—who was still sleeping—to bring him to church, but instead, they had left him asleep on the bed.

When this discovery was made, the unexpected revival began; people began to pray, cry, and call upon the Lord to protect Little Eddie. The Scotts lived ten miles out in the country, and this three-year-old boy was there all alone, which caused concern among the people. How strange it is when people lose control of a situation and fear overcomes their emotions, they will immediately call upon the Lord, and after the crisis is over, they seem to forget their need for the Lord. The Lord did hear and did protect the child until his parents went out and picked him up. He was still asleep on the bed, just like they left him. When they returned to the church, everyone lifted their hands and began to thank the Lord for keeping Little Eddie safe until his parents arrived at the house where he was sleeping. The church service lingered on and on that evening with praise and testimony to the Lord.

> And he sat down, and called the twelve, and saith unto them, If any man desire to be first, the same shall be last of all, and servant of all. And he took a child, and set him in the midst of them: and when he had taken him in his arms, he said unto them, Whosoever shall receive one of such children in my name, receiveth me: and whosoever shall receive me, receiveth not me, but him that sent me. (Mark 9:35–37, KJV)

When Eddie was safely in the arms of his mother, the revival seemed to simmer down a bit, but the thanksgiving continued for a long time afterward.

Seasons of Testing Our Faith

Things that happened in those days of testing would be rather foreign to young ministry today. Betty was pregnant now with Becky; Mike was still in diapers. We had no washing machine, so the old-time rubboard and washpot came back into style at our house. After Becky was born, there was a double load of diapers for Betty to wash on the rubboard and hang out on a clothesline or fence to dry. Many times, when she hung them out to dry, the wind would start blowing; West Texas was known to have sandstorms. When the sand was blowing and the diapers were hung out, they would change color from a bright white to a dingy red. The sand blowing against the diapers, while they were wet or damp, would dye them to a medium-red color. Betty, being the strong mother that she was, never complained about it one time; she would just run them through the water and over the rubboard until the white came back and hang them out again.

On one Friday evening, a church that was in our fellowship in Amarillo was having an area youth rally, and we had some people in our church who wanted to go and carry some of our youth. The sky was looking pretty dark back in the west, with a sandstorm predicted, so my recommendation was for us to cancel our trip to the rally. I was outvoted and outvoted, so we headed toward Amarillo at about five o'clock in the afternoon. The automobile that we were driving was a brand-new 1955 Dodge, a beautiful car. We were into our trip about thirty minutes when the wind began to fiercely blow, and sand filled the air.

All of a sudden, the hood of the car came up and was bent back to the top of the car. I was driving, and this preacher was scared. I couldn't see the road, and at the speed I was driving, it took me several seconds to stop. When we stopped, I said to the owner of the car, "Brother, we need to go back home." I could not believe it, but to my surprise, Brother Goodnight got out of the car, walked over to a wire fence, and found a piece of baling wire. You have to know West Texas to know how difficult it is to find a piece of wire, but he did. He came back to the car, pulled the hood back down, wired it to the car frame, got back into the car, and said, "Let's go to Amarillo."

Well, I have been called ignorant and crazy before, but right then, I was considering just how much truth was in those statements because I felt like this was the most unwise thing I had ever done. We continued our journey, and we took this trip during what was a record sandstorm, the worst ever reported. I could not see the center stripe of the road.

A lady riding with us was plagued with vertigo and began to yell out, "Stop, stop, we are rolling backwards!" The wind was blowing the sand so thick and fast that it seemed to her the car was moving backward. This helped to really shake me up. I found myself on the right shoulder of the highway. I go on record as confessing that the unfolding of God's grace was watching over this car and its occupants. I was doubting that we deserved divine protection at all because of the lack of wisdom we had, but isn't God good? We arrived about ten minutes late for the youth service. When I went to the restroom and looked at my face, I was black with the sand that had settled on my face. After washing up and returning to the auditorium, we entered into a wonderful worship service, where the presence of the Lord became so rich and sweet that it was not long until we had forgotten all about the dangers of our trip and joined with the rest of the church in worship, praise, and Word.

It was difficult to believe that when the service was over and we stepped outside the church that everything was still and quiet. The wind had hushed, and the sand had settled back to the ground. We were very happy then that we had faced the storm and became part of a wonderful evening of worship. Brother Goodnight, the owner of the car, had taught me once again: he that puts his hand and turns back is not worthy of the Kingdom. That night at our home, Betty had to run water over a sheet and hang it over the baby bed where Mike was trying to sleep so that he could breathe: this had been somewhat of a nightmare both at home and on the road.

Try Me, Oh, God!

Testing our faith came in many measures, colors, and sizes. In fact, I wondered if there was any more, but soon, I found out there was plenty to go around and some left over. James 1:2–3 says, "My brother count it all joy when you fall into divers temptations; Knowing this, that the trying of your faith worketh patience" (James 1:2–3 KJV).

One of these trials came driving up one day in a brand-new '56 Chevrolet Bel Air; this was my evangelist who had come for a week's revival. That brand-new Chevy was probably the trial because the first note on it was due, and I'm thinking the evangelist was hoping that note would be made right here at Full Gospel Church. Sure enough, my faith didn't seem to be running too high because I was walking by sight at this time, and my sight was telling me that I didn't have enough people to make a payment on that vehicle. This evangelist is looking for me to gather money enough to make the payment plus. I acted, like, "No problem, brother, we will believe for it to come in."

Well, as I said, my faith wasn't at its best at that time, and by the middle of the week, our offerings were around twenty-five dollars.

The evangelist said, "One day, let's put the seats and lights outside, put up some loudspeakers, and move the revival outside. That way, people will hear the preaching and singing, and our crowds will grow."

With that plan, we proceeded, but you know the people had rather stayed inside, where it was cooler and there were no mosquitoes. Instead of our crowd growing, we lost some of those we had. The handwriting was on the wall now; we were not going to bring in enough finances to make this man's car payment, so he became angry at me. I suggested that we could make about ten dollars a day chopping cotton, but he said, "God didn't call me to chop cotton." I really hate to put this next statement in the book, but I vowed when I began to write that I would tell it like it was, even if it did hurt my pride.

So this preacher boy came so close to punching out the evangelist that there was only maybe an angel's wing that separated us. I became angry enough to fight this guy, and I thought that you didn't even fight before you got saved. Now, I know the Lord had His hand on me and kept me from doing something I would have always regretted the rest of my life, so I apologized and asked him to forgive me for getting angry, which he did. This was a very sad experience because the evangelist had to leave without having enough money for his car payment. He went on to Amarillo, Texas, and held a revival for Brother and Sister Cameron, and the Lord blessed him with an extra amount of money. The revival was very productive, with people being saved and filled with the Spirit. The evangelist really was a great man of God and had a great ministry, but we both had to go through some fiery trials to test our faith.

Well, one test is over; another rises in the horizon. Remember, this is a poor little rich church. Winter came, and being a farming town, the money was scarce. This was a church that paid their pastor with the tithe that came in the Sunday morning service. The procedure was at offering time, a little basket would be set on the altar, and the people would bring their tithe and offering and put it in the basket. Well, this Sunday morning, the basket was set on the altar, but no one stood and came forward. I was sitting on the platform seeing what was happening and thinking, *I don't have any money, and if there is no money put in that basket, I will go home without any money.*

You may have never experienced this, but take it from someone who has: when you are broke, your people has no offering, and you are faced with the responsibility of preaching to this crowd after you pick up the basket without a cent being put in it, God has to come on the scene. He has to show up quick because by this time, you get to wondering, *How am I going to feed my family? How am I going to buy gas so that I can take care of my work?* But joy comes when you do what you are called to do, when you simply stand up, go to the pulpit, open God's Word, and begin to read. Joy comes; nothing else matters. This is the real thing; it is no longer me but it is the Christ that is in me.

It seemed like the tougher the trials became, the richer His grace was poured on. Oh, His grace has no limits, His love has no measure, His power has no boundaries known unto man, but out of His infinite mercies in Jesus, He giveth and giveth and giveth again, amen! Needless to say, Christ got into the message; His anointing came upon me. It didn't matter if there were never any offering as long as I could have this kind of relationship with the Father of my Lord Jesus Christ. In this little poor rich church, God proved himself over and over and over again.

One morning, rather early morning, a furniture truck backed up to our front door, and the man came to the door and asked, "Does the Reverend Billy Shoffner live here?"

My wife answered, "Yes, he does, but we never ordered any furniture."

Well, the man said, "I was told to deliver this furniture to this residence." So the men proceeded to unload a couch and sit it in our living room. They got back into their truck and drove off, leaving Betty standing there, wondering who had sent this. Another time, Betty reached into her purse to get something out and found a rather large bill. She took it out and said, "I wonder who put this money in my purse." This happened another time just when we needed it most. We testified that the Lord put it there, because we had no other explanation. The grace of God was unfolding its mercy and beauty upon our lives.

We experienced several tests while at Wellington. Sometimes, when our family is together, we recall our time at Wellington; we recite the evening that we pulled into a fast-food place and ordered three hamburgers—three, because that was all the money we had to spend. We cut one in half, gave one half to Becky and the other half to Mike, gave thanks for the food and blessed it, and ate. No one complained of not having enough. It reminded me of the miracle of the loaves and fish; everyone ate and had enough.

We spent over a year of ministry at Full Gospel Church and witnessed a revelation of God's Word and a moving of His Spirit like never before or after. It was there the foundation of our faith walk with the Lord was discovered and established, and it has held all these years. Today, the presence and Word is still precious, inspiring, and life-giving. Today, when we recall the blessings and the tests we experienced at the poor little rich church, we always find the blessings received there were much greater and more precious than the trials. Even now in my heart, sometimes I find myself longing to go back to that little white framed church, where we spent so many happy, joyful hours with a people who sincerely loved and respected us. But we must always remember to glean the best fruit and enjoy the riches of its blessings because we will never pass that way ever again.

One Bad Decision

After a year of ministry at the Full Gospel Church, we received an invitation to return to the church that we helped to build in our neighborhood. My dad had given the church the land it was on, and besides that, all our relatives lived close by. This was just too good to be true, and besides, we would be back home. There was just one thing that we didn't remember. The Word of God tells us to pray and get God's will about everything. We were so excited about moving back home that we never thought to seek the will of the Lord about the move. We just accepted the invitation, rented a trailer, loaded up, and headed east. We were so happy to have an opportunity to go home and see Mom and Dad, all our friends and relatives, but we were forgetting the words of Jesus when he said, "A prophet is not without honor, but in is own country, and among his own kin, and in his own house."

Sometimes, we get the idea that we can improve upon the Bible and overcome the principles of the Word. But, friend, please hear this: up until this very hour, it has never happened. The Word of God is supreme, and the world and all things are being held by the power of the Word. If we will not worry about anything but pray about everything with thanksgiving and make our request known to God with thanksgiving, then the peace of God, which passes all understanding, shall keep our hearts and minds through Jesus Christ.

Well, this is the way things fell out for us when we arrived at Faith Temple Church. We started with a bang and thought things were going great. The church began to grow. We were having fantastic services, and suddenly, something beyond our control began to happen. While we were at Wellington Full Gospel, the Lord had given us a revelation of the Christ Life, and it was a message that did not allow us to continue preaching on the flesh issues but more on the spirit. Jesus said, "The flesh profited nothing but the Spirit giveth life," and we had gotten a hold of that revelation and began to minister it above the message of condemnation. We no longer formed our message on how people dressed, how they looked, and we no longer con-demned them for everything, but instead, we preached how they could get deliverance from those habits like drinking, smoking, a lust of the flesh, and all things that opposed the life of Christ.

But they had decided they loved the old wine better than the new, so they closed their hearts to what the Lord had given us to minister. It sounded too easy to them; they didn't have to work for anything under the message of faith and Christ life so that they closed their ears to this message of life. I didn't want to complain to the Lord too much about how we were being treated because I was afraid if I did that, He might say, "It wasn't my idea that you come here. It was your decision." I walked softly before the Lord, fearing what may happen to my family and the ministry, but even when we make bad decisions, God does not turn us away or walk away from us. His wonderful grace continues to unfold before us; soon, we reach the other side of the valley, but this was a long one that I myself had chosen.

One Thursday night, while we were having our service, a man and his wife walked into the church. I looked twice because I was finding it hard to believe it was two of my first church members whom I had pastored at Glad Tidings Tabernacle: none other than Jack and Lois Pither. When I saw them, my heart was made glad, and I began to take courage because I knew these people were people of faith, and wherever they went, something good would happen. So the rest of the service was enriched with the presence of the Lord and with our friends from Mount Pleasant. After the services were finished, we and the Pithers walked out to our house, which was located just a few steps from the church. Lovingly, they revealed to us the backseat of their car was filled with groceries. Jack placed a hundred-dollar bill in my hand and said, "God bless you." Betty and I didn't know how to thank them, because we were like the widow of Elijah's day, with our oil cruse and meal barrel both empty. This was just like heaven had visited us and pulled us out of a big, dark pit.

Betty and I thanked our friends and had prayer, and then Jack said, "Billy, would you like to go to work for me?" I never had to think twice on this one; it was a no-brainer. My answer was, "Yes, and when do I start?" He said, "Come on down when you want, and you can start right away."

Jack had a plumbing business, and a good one, which became one of the best and largest plumbing businesses in Longview, and still is today. It is now owned and operated by his son and grandson. I was not a plumber, but I could be one right now because I was desperate to take care of my family. Becky was about seven months old now and was anemic. We had almost lost her for the lack of medical help, but again, the unfolding grace of God appeared. She spent a night in a Paris hospital paid for by one of Betty's uncles. The next morning, she came out of the hospital looking like a beautiful flower that had just blossomed with all its color; we still praise the Lord God for taking care of her and giving us a beautiful daughter who has a heart for people and finds various ways to minister to them.

Let's go back now to the offer of the plumbing job. The next day, we made arrangements for Betty and the kids to move in with her parents and to live with them until I got a place in Longview and could come after her. So she went to live with her parents while I went a hundred miles southeast to take my next step of faith and whatever the Lord had in store for me to do.

The Miracle Doesn't Stop Here

I moved in with the Pithers; they were not just my friends but also related to me as another father and mother. Jack was my boss, and I was trying to make a plumber and do everything right to please him. Well, I never made a plumber, and Jack knew that well from the very beginning. He wanted to help Betty and me, so he allowed me to stay on until I could find another job. Jack Pither has gone on to be with Jesus, whom he loved and served dearly with all his heart and soul. I will always be grateful for his and Lois's love for me and my family. Lois still lives in Longview and still remains a true friend for life, who calls me every December 29 and wishes me a happy birthday. You see, our birthdays come at the same time, and we always exchange happy-birthday greetings.

The next few days and months of my life were pressing and trying. The experience that I was going through here seemed to be pressing me into a new dimension of life. Up until this time, my entire life was set and focused on the study and ministry of the Gospel, but now, I was moved into a place where my responsibilities seemed to demand working a job and taking care of my family, fully knowing that the ministry that I was called into must continue even if many hours were required of me to work another job. Betty and I had settled on this issue long ago that whatever came into our lives, the ministry of the Word would not ever be forsaken, but it would always be first priority of my life. I remember telling Betty after we had married that ministry would be first place in our lives, and she agreed with me, and that has been our covenant all the years of our marriage.

Change after change began to take place, almost too fast for me to stay abreast of it. We continued to drive back to Faith Temple Church for the weekends, spending Sunday afternoons with Betty's parents, preaching the evening service, and then driving back to Longview, which brought me back to my room at the Pithers around midnight and then to work again on Monday morning. I kept this pace for several weeks then resigned from the church and started seeking out a place to worship in or around Longview. I was not aware at this time that God was working out a long-term plan in the lives of me and my family.

Let me take us back to the little poor rich church that sat on the dusty street of Wellington, Texas. Each morning, after early-morning prayer, I had a special place of prayer in our church, which was just across the street from our house. There was a small basement where I would go to be alone with the Lord to meditate and pray. I always said that little basement was anointed with the Holy Spirit, and I could always enter into the presence of the Lord there.

Well, on this morning, I had a great prayer time, had left the church, and had started walking back to the house when I heard this still small voice in my spirit, and the voice said, "Sabine." Sabine meant absolutely nothing to me, and when I entered the house, I asked Betty, "Have you ever heard the word Sabine or know where it is located?"

Betty answered no, so I got a map and tried to find it on the map, with no success. Sabine, where is Sabine? I knew very well that it was a place because the word came too plain for me to have been mistaken, but we dropped it there and pushed it aside for a long time. When we arrived at Longview, Texas, I began to hear and see the word Sabine. There was a Sabine School not far from Longview and a Sabine River that ran through the south side of Longview. I was excited because I had found the place of the name that came to me while we were in Wellington, Texas.

God's plan sometimes works slow, but it grinds out all the foreign matter and garbage that men allow it to collect. When God is finished, the plan becomes clear and perfect to us. He had been taking me through the wilderness to get me to a place He had destined for me many years before. Isn't God great? Isn't He full of mercy and grace?

Rest assured, my dear reader, He has you in His best interest, and if you will listen and wait for Him to bring to pass His good plan in your life, it may seem to come slow, but it will surely come.

> For I know the thoughts that I think toward you, says the LORD, thoughts of peace and not of evil, to give you a future and a hope. Then you will call upon Me and go and pray to Me, and I will listen to you. And you will seek Me and find Me, when you search for Me with all your heart. (Jeremiah 29:11–13, NKJV)

Pine Grove Assembly

While living in Longview, seeking out a place to serve and minister, I ran across this precious preacher by the last name of Reed. He was pure in heart toward God and was pastoring a little church on the northeast outskirts of Longview. One Saturday, I was out driving and looking for a church. I ran across this church, and Brother Reed happened to be there at the time. I pulled in and met him. We got acquainted, and after visiting and prayer, he told me, "Brother Shoffner, I want you to go with me Saturday night to a church out in the country outside of Beckville, Texas."

I said okay, and the next Saturday night, he picked me up, and we attended service. Well, to say the least, we had a blast; if you understand this kind of language, it just simply means God showed up and the Holy Spirit showed out through the songs, testimonies, gifts of the Spirit, and people rejoicing in the Lord. When we left for home, I felt like I had been to church. Sadly, I state, I wonder how many people today, after being in a church service, feel the joy and peace and really feel like they have been in the presence of the Lord. You know that is what determines a church, if its people are brought into the presence of the Lord.

> And Jacob awaked out of his sleep, and he said, Surely the Lord is in this place, and I knew it not. And he was afraid, and said, How dreadful is this place! This is none other but the house of God, and is the gate of Heaven. (Genesis 28:16–17, KJV)

At Pine Grove Assembly, my heart was captured by the moving of the Spirit of God and the love I felt there in those precious people who worshiped there, so I had to go back on Sunday morning for the services, which were the same. The message was rich and anointed, and the Holy Spirit was moving among the people. I connected with the environment of the spirit of the church, and God used me to speak with the gift of prophesy to the church, which was received with joy. It gave me an introduction into the body of people who served there, and within the next few days, I was called and asked if I would come for a revival, which I was so glad to accept. I had been out of the pulpit much too long now and was anxious to minister the Word of the Lord.

We began revival on a Sunday; contrary to how revivals run today, we were in revival almost three weeks, with each night proving to be fresh and inspiring, with people receiving from the Lord and being renewed in the Holy Spirit. Some received the baptism of the Holy Spirit; some received their healing. There was great joy throughout each night of the revival. I cannot close this chapter without sharing with you readers that funny things happen in the midst of the most spiritual times.

In this revival, there was a young man attending who was much anointed and very zealous for the Lord. One evening in the service, this young man was moving about in a dance before the Lord, and there was a lady kneeling at the altar, praying. She was paying no attention to what was going on with the young man, but he happened to come by her and bumped into her. She began to fall over. I was standing behind the pulpit, looking on, when this happened; the lady looked up to see if anyone was watching and was embarrassed she saw me. I had a big Texas grin on my face that I could not control, and she saw that I was grinning, and began laughing with me. When it was over, the two of us had something to remember for the rest of our lives.

We all called this lady Meme, and she became one of our lifelong friends. We pastored her for all the years she lived. The final result of the revival was that I was invited to come and pastor the church. I gladly accepted and was there for a year, and then I moved on to our next tenure and to experience another unfolding of God's precious grace.

A Three-Year Revival

Strange and unusual things fall out into our lives when we are following the leadership of the Holy Spirit. It is like when the nation of Israel was following the cloud by day and the pillar of fire by night. They were covered and protected each day by God's covering of grace. The waters rolled back so that they could make their escape from the Egyptians; the rock that followed them through the wilderness split and gave water for all the people and their animals. Heaven's manna fell at each dawn of day to give food to all the people of God; many other miracles happened along the way to sustain the people on their journey to the Promised Land that God had promised to give them.

However, the people did not take advantage of God's promises and grace by disobeying and not believing God's Word, so many of them died in the wilderness because of unbelief. This journey that the Lord has set before you and me will someday find its destination, and it depends largely upon us as to where this journey will carry us. The way we respond to the things God allows to come into our lives will determine our destination at the end of the journey. John 3:16 says, "God so loved the world that he gave his own begotten son that whosoever believeth in him shall not perish but will have everlasting life" (KJV). Let's make sure that we embrace God's love and His plan of salvation, so when our travels end here, we will spend eternity with Christ our King.

While living in the city of Longview at 110 South King Street, we met with some very serious occasions and some very humorous ones. The most trying times we had relative to our ministry sometimes brought us to our knees, seeking the Lord for a solution to the problem, and Jesus never fails because He is aware and concerned with those things related to his children. But the more humorous events were about our children.

One summer day, when the grass was fresh and green with the refreshing rains, Becky and Mike were outside playing and having a huge time just being outside and having the freedom to run and play when, out of the blue, they got this beautiful idea about giving something to their mother. You see, all the flowers were blooming, colorful, and beautiful. Our next-door neighbors, Mr. and Mrs. King, had a gorgeous bed of red flowers right at the back of their garage. Our children thought how much their mother would appreciate their thoughtfulness by receiving a bouquet of those beautiful flowers, so they proceeded over to Mrs. King's house, broke off a handful of the flowers, and carried them inside, where they found Betty taking care of her housework. They presented them to her with a big smile, thinking she would be so proud of their gift.

But to their sad surprise, Mom did not receive them with a smile. Instead, as soon as she thought where they had picked them, she became very angry and explained to them that they were not to take other people's flowers without permission, and she said to them very firmly, "Take the flowers back to Mrs. King and apologize to her for taking her flowers." In my mind, I see them now and their unwillingness to carry out this command of their mother; nevertheless, Mike and Becky reluctantly walked slowly back to the Kings' house, handed the flowers to Mrs. King, and made their apologies to her. Surely there was a tear in Mrs. King's eye, because she really loved the kids and did not think this act of apology was necessary. But even so, she accepted the flowers and their apologies for taking them. Mrs. King also told Betty that it would not have been necessary for the kids to have brought them back. As I remember back, I think there was a note of sorrow in each of our hearts; nevertheless, we all learned a great lesson of forgiving and never taking what is not ours.

While living at 110 South King Street, my job was just around the corner from where we lived when you make a right turn on Nelson Street. There was the TSPA warehouse where I worked for approximately three years. One day, I became deathly sick with the flu, so sick that I had to leave the job and go home. When I reached home, I immediately went to bed. When I am sick, I don't want any visitors and take no calls; I just want to be alone and left alone. But Betty didn't have that same concept, so she got on the phone and called our friends Brother Jack Pither and his mother-in-law, Myrtle Moncy, to come and pray for me. When I discovered she had called someone to come, I scolded her for calling them; I was sick and didn't want to see anyone.

You must bear with me. You see, I believe and preach that Jesus still heals, and now, it seems that I am denying what I believe. I am so thankful that our Father in heaven has grace and patience with His children, for if He did not, I would have been gone many years ago.

Back to our visitors. Jack Pither and Myrtle Moncy also are people of faith and know how to pray and touch the Lord for others. A miracle just walked through the door and to my bed, where I was lying. No time was wasted; Jack and Myrtle knelt very humbly and began to pray in a very simple way, just like they were talking directly to God Himself. With their hands laid on me, they prayed for maybe five minutes, rose up from prayer, said good-bye, and left. Many times, we do not realize when a miracle takes place until awhile later, and then it suddenly dawns on us we have received a miracle.

This was the case with this miracle of healing that I had received through prayer. The prayer was so causal, so quiet, and so short that it seemed as nothing had happened, but our God doesn't come with fanfare. He comes many times in a still, small voice and hardly makes himself known to man. But, beloved, He is always there, always loving and caring for His children. Just place your trust in Him, and He will change your life from death to life, from sadness to joy, from sickness to health, and from darkness to light, because he is the light of the world. He has come to give us life and to give abundantly.

Shortly after prayer, I discovered that I was not sick anymore; I felt well and was ready to get up and start working. Betty happened to be putting up window curtains, so I got up and began to help her with the curtains. I was healed; I was whole. Jesus had come to my house and touched me through His servants, and again, Betty and I witnessed another miracle of God. Oh, my friends, please don't allow anyone to persuade you to believe that Jesus doesn't heal anymore or that He doesn't perform miracles anymore. He is just the same Lord Jesus as He was when He walked the streets of Jerusalem, when His voice could be heard as it rang out over the stormy waters of Galilee, as He stood up in the boat with the unbelieving disciples. Yes, my beloved, Jesus is the same. The only difference in Him now as then is that He can be with all of us at the same time, and He can love and tend to His flock wherever they may be in the world.

I mentioned strange and unusual things happen when we follow the cloud and the fire. When Betty and I resigned and left Pine Grove Assembly Church, we were living in Longview. We had resigned on a Sunday morning, and the next Sunday morning, we had found no place to attend church. However, we had gotten up as usual and gotten ready for church when a knock was heard at the door. When I arose to see who was there, I saw it was, to my surprise, a young man from a church in Kilgore, Texas.

When he came inside, he asked us, "Where are you going to church today?" And our answer was, "We don't know, we were just planning on driving around until we found a church that we thought we might want to attend."

At this, the young man said, "Why don't you come over to Kilgore and preach for us today?"

Betty and I glanced quickly at each other, and with a nod of approval, we agreed. Why not? We had no place to go, so we followed this young man to Kilgore and to a small church located on Highway 31 on the outskirts of North Kilgore. At this juncture of our thinking back, I am reminded of the time when the scripture says, in John 4:4, "And he must need go through Samaria." Now that I look back at this time of our ministry, I know perfectly well that the Lord had ordained our position and was using a method of getting us there that neither of us was mindful of.

Let's stop awhile and think about the time when the Holy Spirit had spoken to me the word Sabine, of which I had no clue why. The Heavenly Father had purpose for Jesus to travel through a place that was really off-limits for Him to go; there in Samaria was a thirsty woman who needed a drink of living water. Jesus needed to carry this living water to her. Furthermore, there were hundreds more Samaritans who needed to drink from that same well of water that Jesus made available. So now we see there were people in Kilgore who were thirsty for living water and the Holy Spirit. The Lord was getting me, slowly but surely, closer to that place named Sabine; I found out soon after we had arrived at Calvary Lighthouse that there was a school and community close by with the name Sabine! The grace of God was still unfolding, but I was not yet able to understand how or why.

The name of the church was Calvary Lighthouse. That first Sunday morning, we met with around fifteen people. The Lord was gracious to us by blessing the people with His presence; it was almost like we were at home and very comfortable worshiping there with the people of Calvary. We were invited back for the evening service, and we accepted. We were called to be their pastor, and for three years, the Holy Spirit met with us in a very special way each service. Our services turned out to be like revival services each time that we met.

Over the period of three years, we witnessed the church growing in number and spirit. People were saved and baptized with the Holy Spirit; we witnessed many healings and God's grace was marvelously manifested in many ways. As I glance back now, I wouldn't take anything for my journey now and our time spent with the precious people at Calvary Lighthouse and the many blessings that came our way while we ministered there.

The Vision Becomes Clearer

I must be truthful with you readers concerning some events that seem to not be avoidable when you follow the plans that God has for you. The closure and resigning of our tenure at Calvary was far from being pleasant. The completion of our pastorate at Calvary Lighthouse was like this: a very young church in Carthage, Texas, that had begun under the ministry of Brother Mark Beard had invited us to minister a service or two. Our ministry was well received, so they had invited us for a revival meeting. Since my ministry consists largely of an evangelistic style, I couldn't resist the invitation for a revival.

The revival turned out to be exceptionally good; people were coming and enjoying the singing and preaching of the Word. People were responding to the invitations given for salvation, so the church decided that another week would be productive for the church. We continued for another week. In the event of two weeks of revival at Carthage, it took us away from our two Sunday services at Calvary Lighthouse. When I returned back to our church, I was met by our church board of men who informed me upfront that they were not pleased with their pastor being out of their pulpit on Sunday mornings.

I was young and ignorant; I now say this truthfully and humbly with tears. Instead of reconciling this matter in love and prayer, I became demanding of my time, and I would use it as the Lord led me. Our Lord does not govern with that kind of attitude but with unity and love. I must confess that I was wrong and lost the battle on the ground where I stood, but I learned a lesson that I will never have to take that course again—no, never! The final results of that board meeting was this: I resigned from my pastorate with a hurt and accusative spirit and walked away leaving people feeling hurt and sad because of all the goodness we had enjoyed together was gone and could never be restored again. When I had searched my heart and the Lord had so gently reproved me, I was restored in my relationship with the Lord and continued on my journey of ministry.

It Is Time to Put Down Roots

I sense a feeling of weariness come over me now as I think of the next fifty years of the valleys and mountains I must cross with the writing of my memory, searching out the experiences both good and bad, and still being aware there will be many things of importance that my mind will not be able to remember. If you have been so kind to have traveled with me along till now, I trust you to bear with me as we continue our journey of the unfolding grace of His love. Our desire is that reviewing the next fifty years of the Lord's work will accomplish two things: first, that the Lord will be honored and magnified, and second, that you, my reader, will be blessed with the many occasions and experiences we will try to share with you.

Yes, at the age of thirty-one, Betty and I felt it was time to put down roots and begin to accomplish some permanent plans for the life of our family. At first, the church at Carthage looked somewhat shaky because after three months of working and pastoring the people, we had not seen any growth at all, so we spoke to the church and resigned from our place of pastor, thinking the Lord would bring someone else along who could help the church grow. I spent the next three months at my job in Longview as warehouseman, and also, I had several revivals lined up that I wanted to preach. It so happened that I had a good boss at my manual job who would allow me to take off time to go out and preach meetings. I saw that my boss had favor with God and respected the ministry that I was involved in.

By the month of December, we had covered about all our meetings and were having some downtime in ministry when we received a call from Carthage. The church, Northside Assembly, had not found a pastor yet; they asked if we would please come and preach for them until they find one. I was rather glad to get back into the pulpit, so my answer was yes, we will come. When we met with the people of Northside Assembly—that was the name of the church at that time—we had a little meeting, and this was the agreement we made with the church that we will be their pastor until they find one. I don't think I stopped to consider very thoroughly my answer, but nevertheless, that was it. I was there until a pastor came and was set into that office.

Almost forty years has lapsed, and I am still pastoring. The church is now Northside Christian Center (NCC). It is here that we put down roots that lived and brought forth fruit in its time; it is here where the valleys become deep and dreary and the mountains sometimes were too high for us to climb. When you put down roots for Jesus, nothing can move you away from those roots.

The Rubber Hits the Road

I am sure you are acquainted with the term "When the rubber hits the road," and then you discover what kind of material the tires are made from. In this case, the material had to be tough and durable, for the road was not an easy one. While we were away from the church from July to December, the church had progressed from having church in the old Esquire Theater building to a huge dwelling house located at 414 North Saint Mary. This house was rather unique as it was built at the beginning of the 1900s. It had ten rooms, two bathrooms, and a large hall all the way down through the middle. This house was ideal for having church; plus, it made a living quarter for the pastor and the family for the first year of our stay at the Northside Christian Center.

We praised God for the accomplishment of the church purchasing this property, but it is difficult to describe the many encounters you can have living in the same building that people are using for a church, Oh, now we count it all with joy as we look back, but try looking at it from the front side and see if it generates very much joy. You completely lose your privacy around church time; people must use the phone and don't feel like they need to ask the use of it. People have to use the bathroom, and ours was accessible to everyone. You were even blessed with uninvited guests at times for lunch, so be ready at all times, for you know not what hour you might have visitors. You are thinking these are complaints, but not really, it just went with the territory, and we were blessed all along the way.

When the Old Becomes New

Remember, the house had a large hall down the middle of it. This was ideal for a nice little auditorium, so the men of the church moved the north side wall back and the south side wall back a few feet and replaced them, which gave us a room twenty-five feet wide and about fifty feet long. We had a preacher friend who was a pastor at Highway Tabernacle near Timpson and a good carpenter and a very good friend who came and finished out the inside of the auditorium. Brother Gene Lewis was our preacher friend's name, and he remains to be a great friend till this very day. We placed theater seats in for seating purposes, wainscoted the walls with knotty pine paneling, and painted out the Sheetrock; it became a beautiful little church that we enjoyed worshiping in for around three years. We were a church on the move, so this church building did not exist very long until the Lord began to tug and pull at our hearts to rise up and build, and rise up and build we did.

Number-Two Building Program

The old house place that we had renovated and built a sanctuary had become too small for our congregation, and besides, our people wanted a more church house appearance, so the Lord began to tug at our hearts once again to rise up and build. I suppose building has become a trademark of ministry for us because almost everywhere we pastor, there is something for us to build, and we love to get involved in building for the Lord.

We feel that this time element of NCC was a very vital and important part of its history. First of all, the founders of the church made up the main church body and were very faithful in their attendance and giving. Again, we met with financial problems because the church was small at first, but this problem was soon overcome. NCC had people who were so loyal to their pastor that they would sacrifice their giving, even borrowing money to make up our weekly salary. We will always be grateful to those who stood with us in our times of need.

The unfolding of God's wonderful grace never ceased or departed from us. Many times, NCC's members would bless us in different ways. It was one of those times when our need was great; we had just sat down for lunch when a knock came at our kitchen door. When I went to see who it was, one of the ladies from the church was standing there and said, "The Lord told me to give this to you." And with that said, she laid a hundred-dollar bill in my hand. Even now, my eyes fill with tears of joy when I remember the acts of some of the NCC people whom I will forever be indebted to. I would like to be more personal by writing their names, but maybe it would not be profitable at this time, and besides, they would not want any praise for their gifts of love. We bonded very closely to the founders of NCC, and until this day, they are some of our dearest friends even if it seemed right for us to part ways for a while.

As the tug at our hearts concerning building became stronger, we began to talk and discuss this among the church members. At one Sunday-evening service, the Lord laid a message on my heart with the title of One-Man Building Program. Ah, I will never forget that night service. I preached it with a prophetic anointing, telling how God spoke to Noah to build an ark to the saving of his household and how, "by faith, Noah, being warned of God of things not seen as yet, moved with fear, prepared an ark to the saving of his house." I wasn't quite sure anyone else was getting the message, but I was and knew the Lord was telling us it is time to rise up and build. I found out the next day that another man received the message and moved on it.

I was working at TSPA in Longview at that time, had just gotten in from work, and had sat down to have supper when one of our members came in and couldn't wait to give me a message. He said, "Do you know there is a man over at your church with a hammer and crowbar tearing down your preaching place?"

"No," I said. "But as soon as I finish dinner, I will be right over to help him tear it down."

You see, the Word of God is powerful and doesn't return without accomplishing what it is sent to do. This man, Brother Ed Mayhaw, had heard the message of the one-man building program, and he actually began to apply the message that he had heard to his life. The work for a new church building had begun at that very moment. The Word had not returned void of fruit. Our churches would become powerful and compelling if its people would begin to be doers of the Word instead of just hearers. Jesus tells us in Matthew 7:21 (KJV), "Not every one that saith unto me, Lord, Lord, shall enter into the Kingdom of Heaven, but he that doeth the will of my Father which is in heaven."

Time and space will not allow me to cover all or even most of the details concerning the tearing down and rebuilding of a new white-brick church, but we will hit the highlights because this was also "the unfolding of God's grace" in a very different realm.

It seemed that we always needed money, and money was kind of hard to come by at that time. So again, we began to pray and believe the Lord to help us by showing us how we could get the funds that were needed to build. We overlook the most simple things when it comes to receiving from God. All the promises are there, and all you and I have to do is to believe and ask for them and then do what is required of us. In this case of needing funds for building, it meant everyone working and doing their part, and we had some people who were ready for that to begin. When we tried to borrow money to build, the first question the lender would ask us was how much the church has in their building fund, and our reply to that was there was none. If our church had money in reserve, we would not be trying to borrow. We would have begun building with whatever amount we had.

Well, that was before I became acquainted with the system, so we simply didn't use the system in this building program. We created our own system, and you know what? It worked, because the grace of God was in force, and we can do all things through Christ Jesus who strengthens us. There is no limit to the power of God through faith in His grace; no power on earth or under the earth can withstand the power of God's grace through faith. One day, He will prove this to the entire world and every living creature therein.

In order for us to supply most of our lumber for the new building, the old one we had torn down had enough and some left over, and it was choice pine heart lumber in the measurements of all lengths and widths. This material, which was taken out of the old building, began to be placed into the new church building. This truth began to be disclosed: the old was becoming new again. This is what God does in the heart of the believer when the believer starts putting their faith and trust into Jesus Christ. As we receive Him into our life, the old becomes new, and there is a restoration of an old man becoming new again. "Therefore if any man be in Christ, he is a new creature: old things are passed away; behold, all things become new" (2 Corinthians 5:17, KJV).

There were hard oak seals for the foundation. As we removed the lumber from the old building, we would clean it, pull out the nails—remember, they were square nails—and stack the lumber. One of our oldest and dearest members by the name of Brother Jim Daily would sit in a chair. Because of health issues, he was not able to stand. For hours, he would sit and pull nails as we would bring the lumber close enough to him for him to reach. His life was Christ centered, his faith was strong, and his vision was like that of Abraham. Yes, he was looking for that city whose builder and maker is God. His God did not disappoint him for he found it and is now dwelling in its glory with Jesus being his eternal life.

In a few months, the old building was torn down, and the lumber cleaned up. We were ready to start up with a new building. While the men were tearing down and cleaning the lumber of the old building, the ladies of the church were busy fund-raising.

Praise God for Our Ladies

This section of our story highlights a message to shine into generations to come. It is a message of "Whatever your hands find to do, do it with all your might." Again, be ye doers of the Word and not hearers only. There were ladies in NCC who believed they could make a difference by applying the work principle to this part of our church, so they bonded together in agreement that each month, or maybe twice a month, to have a dinner of chicken, dressing, and ham with all the trimmings for the townspeople. They used the United Gas company house, the community house in the park, to serve the people. They were very faithful and consistent with what they did, and I might add that these ladies knew how to cook so that people would come to get a good home-cooked meal. "Feed them, and they will come" was our motto at that time.

This fund-raising project continued for a long time, and God blessed it. The people of Carthage were faithful to come eat with us. Lasting relationships were built from this fund-raising effort so that even now, those who still remain remember those days when they enjoyed a good home-cooked meal prepared by the ladies of Northside Christian Center. My job was to deliver meals to people who would call in. Sometimes, my car would be full of dinners, and I would carry them to the people who had called in.

Let me take you back to the time when the Lord spoke prophetically to the church concerning building this house: "I will roll the water back a little at a time. You will not see the completion all at once, only a few steps at a time, but I, the Lord, will keep the water rolled back that you can continue your work until it is finished."

Let me share with you how the Lord fulfilled this Word. We had some volunteer work but had to pay a carpenter who knew how to build. When we began the building, enough money was supplied to finish the roof. Then when the brickwork started, there were enough funds to finish the brickwork. Every time a new project came up, the money for that project was available, just like the Lord said. Not all at once, but as we moved forward and worked, the Lord kept the supply of materials ready to go into the building. It was until the building was completed, and the people moved in. Indeed, we saw God's grace unfolding toward a new white-brick church for the people of NCC to worship in.

While the church was under construction, the people again were like Israel when she was wandering in the wilderness. I am reluctant to say this, but we had fun in the wilderness. The manna fell each day, but so did the trials and pressures. Since we had to find a place to worship, we chose an old restaurant building near the church location to hold our services in. This was kind of nice, had plenty of room, and served well as a sanctuary, but like Israel, our camping here was brief, and then we had to move to another camping place. This was a blessing because this facility was given over to the people who gave out groceries to those who needed food. We had to move again, and this time, it was to a facility that had been used by a doctor here. It was a clinic building where all sorts of vitamins were used, so the whole place smelled like a vitamin. When church was over, you felt like you had visited the doctor.

In the clinic, our sanctuary had downsized from a 30 × 40 feet to 4 × 25 feet. The piano was set off into another room next to the auditorium for lack of space, so we couldn't see the pianist from the sanctuary. The song leader had to communicate from the church to the next room to let the pianist know what song to play. We spent months serving in this location, and some of the people grew weary and turned back. But those who had set their minds and hearts to see the finished work hung in there, and the Lord continued to make His grace known by sustaining us with people and a place to worship.

We Reached the Land

The day that we moved into the new church facility, these words could be heard plainly among the people: "We have reached the Promised Land." Well, that remained to be seen, but at least we felt like our wilderness journey had ended, and we had moved into a permanent dwelling, which completed our journey for a while. We first moved into the youth room, which we called the CA room at that time. It was large enough to hold all the people and the piano. We rejoiced in the Lord that we were back on the property the Lord had given us, and our services were rich and sweet.

After several months, the church auditorium had been finished and was ready to be used. The first service held in the new sanctuary was preached by Brother Elvie Adams; it was a great message and carried the theme Motivation, or How to Be Motivated. That was one of those messages that remain in my mind until this very day. This message was preached on Sunday, December 26, 1965. Brother Adams still lives here in Carthage and is being a great blessing to the people of Panola County through the work that he is involved in.

A New Dimension Lies Ahead

The Northside Christian Center began to observe the unfolding of God's grace in new dimensions of growth and ministry. Change, however you spell it, is not easy for some of us, and that is exactly what the Lord began to require. When we become familiar with a certain way of doing things and with a certain territory, it is frightening to have to make a change into something that we have never experienced before. You may rest assured that those three disciples—Peter, James, and John—sensed a certain fear when Jesus said, "Men, I want you to take a walk with me today." Instead of a walk, it was a climb, a climb up a mountain they had never climbed before. These three disciples knew something was up because Jesus chose only three out of twelve to walk with him; what could it be? They already knew this man Jesus did awesome things, like speaking to the wind to hush, speaking to the troubled water to be calm, speaking to the dead to rise up—wow! What could be on the agenda today? However, they felt honored to have been chosen to go with him, and the journey began.

At first, at the base of the mountain was a thick growth of underbrush that they had to press and search a way through. The unknown always holds a sense of fear to those who walk into it. Not knowing what this walk consisted of, the three disciples were very anxious to get past the thickets and underbrush and to come out into the open clear freshness of the mountain breeze. If we could have heard them speaking to Jesus, it might have been something like this: "Master, how much farther do we have to go until we reach the other side?" Or "Do you think we may encounter danger from wild animals while in this maze of underbrush?" Jesus probably answered, "Be not afraid, I assure you the journey is nearing the end." And suddenly, light broke through the darkness. The sunlight fell upon their faces, and sighs of relief and praise came forth. They had conquered the unknown.

While making this journey, there will be many unknown places that we must conquer, but if Jesus is with us, the victory is always ours. The disciples overcame the dangers that lay at the base of mountain and came out into the clearing. And behold, at the top, they experienced a dimension of God's glory that had never been experienced by man before. They saw Jesus glorified, standing with Moses and Elijah, which left them speechless—well, almost speechless; Peter must have felt that he was obligated to speak. As at many times before, he said the wrong thing.

In order to reach the fullness of God's grace, it always takes us through change after change. If we never undergo the challenge of change, we will never reach the height of God's plan for our lives. We must notice in this great event the disciples experienced, Jesus only chose three out of twelve. This tells us that only a few will meet the challenges of change. Only a few will follow Jesus through the difficult places, but it also discloses to us that only a few will see the fullness of Christ's glory and be filled with the knowledge that those who died in faith are still living. At the will of God, they can return and stand upon this earth in a glorified body. This manifestation of the Father's glory was so special that He would not allow Peter, James, and John to disclose the revelation of transfiguration until He had risen from the dead.

When Jesus invites you to take a walk with Him, you may not know exactly where it will lead, but remember three things: you are one of the few He chooses to walk with Him, He knows that you will faithfully finish the course, and praise God, you can know without a doubt that He has something very special to share with you. Even with the change, no matter how impossible it may seem to be, just know that the One who can do the impossible is walking with you and that He has a purpose for you making the walk that transforms. Time and space will not allow us to share with you those who have gone on record, those who took that walk with God, and glorious things took place in their lives. For instance, Enoch walked with God and was not, for God took him home with him. Noah walked with God, saved his household, and became the heir of righteousness just by building an ark. God's servants should always be ready to take up the cross and follow Jesus through the valleys and over the mountains.

Changes That Make a Difference

Change sometimes can become fearful because it rearranges everything that is already set in place and has been that way forever, or at least for Northside. Let's start with the change of ministry. Ministry began to take on a new fresh spirit of love and grace. It seemed as the people began to gather for worship that there was a soft, cool breeze beginning to blow upon the congregation. The ministry began to change, from seeking new revelation and new sermons to preaching in a flow of God's love and grace, ministering to the entire congregation. Up until this time, the ministry seemed to reach only a few people, and those few were blessed.

Some of the new revelations did not reach the entire assembly. We would have new people come in and not be able to grasp the message that was going forth, so the Holy Spirit began to deal with us to cast a net of God's love and compassion over the service, which allowed everyone to feel they were being received and ministered to. Please understand that there are no compromises in a true message of love and grace, so we were not giving up the truth so that we could bring in numbers. Nevertheless, the number began to increase, and soon, our church was filled with new people who were hungry for the life of Jesus Christ. The change of ministry had begun.

God's Love and Life Makes Satan Uncomfortable

As changes began to occur in the ministry and worship, the Spirit of the Lord became stronger and more intensified with the conviction of sin, and our enemy, Satan, became uncomfortable during the services. On an Easter morning, after worship and praise, we began our message on the resurrection life of Christ. As the anointing became very heavy and the people began to be ministered to through the Word of God, there was a young man in the congregation who began to twist and turn and move about. This young man had become obsessed with an evil spirit and could not bear the presence of the Lord with a spirit of Satan.

As he continued to twist and turn and move about, four or five people from the congregation stood up, quietly walked over to this young man, laid their hands on him, and began to pray; suddenly, he screamed out, and the spirit left him. He relaxed and was very calm; Jesus had set him free. Where the Spirit of the Lord is, there is freedom, and evil spirits cannot remain in the presence of God's Spirit. At the close of the service, this young man stood, asked for permission to speak, and came to the front of the church. He began to testify that he had become a Christian several months ago, but he had previously been a Buddhist. While practicing that religion, he became demon obsessed, but his words were "This morning, Jesus set me free." This young man soon became a minister of the Word of God.

Not many years after this deliverance, we were having a revival with Pastor J. L. Dutton, and at the closing of his message, an invitation was given for prayer to anyone who had a need. A young man, around nineteen years old, came up for prayer, and as we began to pray for him, he started pulling away from us. Suddenly, he broke to run out of the church; as he did, I made my first tackle in church. I literally caught him and brought him to the floor, where we began to pray for him; as we prayed, the spirit loosened him and came out. The man was set free and came back many times to worship at NCC and gave his testimony of deliverance from the enemy. Mark 16:17B says, "In my Name they shall cast out devils." We find that the demonic spirits are still hanging around today, but the power of our God will take charge of them and cast them out.

Baptisms Can Be Dangerous

At the early dawning of Northside Christian Center, we would have water baptisms quite often. We had not built a baptistery in the new church yet, so we had to use a pool or lake for our baptizing services. As I share this with you, I chuckle under my breath because we witnessed one of the most unusual baptisms ever. Maybe it could have made the record if it had been known. It was a warm Sunday afternoon, about two o'clock, when most of the church members gathered at Mr. Poss's stock pond. This was a nice little pond that served as a watering place for all the livestock. Mr. Poss ran a large number of cattle, which were always grazing around the stock pond; most of the cattle were Brahma.

As we were preparing for the baptism, no attention was given to the cows that grazed around the pool. Our group was well protected from the cattle coming near us because the place where we were baptizing was fenced off and a bridge connected the fence. What we didn't notice was that the bridge was open; we had not parked a car on it, so the cattle had passage to where we were. Suddenly, before anyone noticed, there stood a Brahma bull as big as a freight car, and he was headed straight toward the water's edge.

When he reached the edge of the water, he quickly turned around and began snorting and pawing up dirt.

At first, we were spellbound, not knowing what to do, where to run or stand our ground. Well, we chose the latter. One precious lady by the name of Ellison had an umbrella in her hand and began going toward the bull, slinging the umbrella at the bull. It reminded me of David encountering Goliath in battle; the only difference was the bull was still standing and pawing and snorting as to say, "This is my territory, and I dare anyone to take it from me."

Brother J. C. Mangham, a committed and faithful member of the church, was at the baptism service and was wearing a dark-red shirt; as I glanced at the bull and at J. C., I noticed the bull looking at the red shirt. I whispered softly to my brother and said, "That bull is looking directly at your red shirt, and if I were you, I believe I would move." Although he was a rather slow-moving man, right then, he changed gears and moved quickly away from the bellowing bull.

We had one wise man among us; he was a rather small-built man but used wisdom. He walked up close to the bull and reached out his hand, as if to have something in it to eat, and the bull stopped snorting and began to follow Albert, the man, up the pool band right out on the bridge and walked on to the other side of the bridge and fence. Someone drove their car upon the bridge and parked it there, where the bull could not come back over; everyone breathed a sigh of relief. The old Brahma crossed the bridge and trotted on down the road.

Some days later, someone was telling Mr. Poss about our encounter with his Brahma bull; at hearing this, his face looked very serious and said, "That is a mean bull. You were very fortunate that someone didn't get hurt." We were doing business for our Heavenly Father, so again, we witnessed an amazing account of our Father's grace unfold before our eyes and went about our baptizing with the joy of the Lord.

When Family Offers Strength

After sixty years of pastoral ministry, my family has been perpetually blessed to witness the unfolding of God's wonderful grace in our lives and the life of the church. I am now beginning to understand the grace of God working and providing strength and encouragement through a family's love and support. It suddenly dawned upon me that God had given me one of the greatest and most vital gifts that a preacher can ever hope for: a family who loves one another, loves and respects God and parents, and who stands with you through any kind of problem that may arise in a church setting. And believe me, church problems come as long as people fill the pews and preachers take their stand behind the pulpit. Problems are inevitable. This is when only a loyal and loving family can reach out to you in a way that God has provided for preachers. You can always count on their loving care. Jesus said, "In the world you will have tribulation: but be of good cheer, I have overcome the world."

Right up front, I want to make my declaration and stand that Jesus Christ has given me a wife and three great children whom my whole life is built upon and around. Michael Lynn is my firstborn whose integrity as a man and whose strength and faithfulness come from God. Mike has earned a good report by remaining faithful in his serving God and family; I am now drawing much of my strength from his life. Rebecca Ann is my pride and joy because she reflects the love and compassion of God to others and shows great respect to her family and to the church. I always feel I honor her when I introduce her to someone by saying, "This is my favorite daughter," and everyone understands and agrees that Becky is loved by many people. There is David Glynn, our second son, who was born into the Shoffner family seven years after Rebecca and whom I consider the pillar of the family. He is strong in his opinions, stands strong in defense of what he loves and knows is right, and has a deep love for the Lord and God's house. David has worked hard to educate himself to be able to meet the challenges of this changing world and has become a great asset to our society.

David—the psalmist, the king of Israel, and God's shepherd—describes and evaluates family better than any writer that has set the pen to writing. I share his love and evaluation of family at this time:

> Children are a gift from God; they are his reward. Children born to a young man are like sharp arrows to defend him. Happy is the man who has his quiver full of them. That man shall have the help he needs when arguing with his enemies. (Psalm 127:3–5)

> Your wife shall be contented in your home. And look at all those children! There they sit around the dinner table as vigorous and healthy as young olive trees. That is God's reward to those who reverence and trust him. May the Lord continually bless you with heaven's blessings as well as with human joys. May you live to enjoy your grandchildren! And may God bless Israel! (Psalm 128:3–6)

> May our sons flourish in their youth like well-nurtured plants. May our daughters be like graceful pillars, carved to beautify a palace. (Psalm 144:12)

Writings from My Children

By the time that I was born, I had already heard approximately 100 sermons. I figured three per week for thirty-six weeks, and this did not include Friday night youth rallies or weekly revivals. After church at night, we would ride home listening to XERF, a powerful radio station in Del Rio, Texas. Every night, there were preachers back to back for the ride home. Most seemed to have initials like A.A. Allen, J.C. Hibbard, and then there were Lester Rollof, Oral Roberts, and many more that I can't remember. Becky and I were in the backseat, her in the floorboard (we didn't know about carbon monoxide back then, so maybe that's why she's a little dizzy sometimes) and me laid across the backseat; of course, we didn't have seat belts then either. We would sing each program's theme song, like "Rescue the Perishing," and then we would fall asleep when the message began. I never knew if Dad turned on this station to learn or to put us to sleep.

I am now 58 years old, have heard thousands of sermons, and am not worse for wear. I have been blessed by having the privilege to hear, learn, and grow because of the exposure to the Word. I can tell you for sure that I am partial to my Dad's preaching, even the reruns. He is not only a good preacher and a humble servant, but he is the best Dad ever!

Mike

December 1997

Dear Mom and Dad,

As I was taking the lights off our tree, I thought how wonderful it is to be able to put them away for another year, but be able to keep the "one" which we had celebrated near us every day of our lives. I want to thank you for all the gifts you gave me and all of our family, but most of all for the gift you have passed down to me, Mike, and David, that we can keep on passing it on down to our children. An inheritance we can enjoy right now without giving y'all up to receive it. I feel like I have my cake and get to eat it too. Without y'all sharing spiritual knowledge with us and "living" it, we could not have had a foundation under us that is solid. My foundation has been tested, shaken, and retested, and it is still holding! This I can pass on to my children. I have already shared this with them, and all three of them have expressed gratitude for it here lately. I hope everyone of them keeps passing it on and on. There is not a greater gift that y'all could have given us kids.

Your favorite Daughter,
Becky

Hear, See and Do: Lessons from My Dad

Growing up as a "Preacher's Kid," I was blessed with multiple chances every week to hear the Good News of the Gospel. I'm sure there were plenty of times over the years that Dad thought that this seed or that principle didn't take root, but Dad, faith starts with hearing. Dad set that foundation for all of us kids and for that I am so thankful! The best news of all is that he didn't stop there, and whether he realized it or not, how he has lived life has allowed us to not just hear, but to see love in action and to know the right thing to do when situations arise.

I recall a late night tap on the door and a young man with his family in the car. They were traveling and had no money for food. Dad put on his shoes and said, "Follow me to the grocery store." Sometime later I asked him why he didn't just give them some money to buy groceries as they continued their trip. His answer was practical, not just spiritual, "When you give someone money, you never know exactly what they will spend it on and if the need is really being met." I had heard the sermons about giving the hungry food or the cold your coat and understood the basic Biblical concept, but watching Dad demonstrate those passages over the years brought reality to the scripture.

Years later, this lesson flashed vividly in my mind when one Sunday morning an elderly gentleman in poor health came to our local church in Weaver, Alabama. When he asked for some money for food, my immediate response was, "I'll take you to the store and help you unload the groceries at your house." I had no idea what I was walking into, but if I hadn't went to the home, I would have never known how bad this family's living conditions were. Conditions that had deteriorated the gentleman's health to the point that he died shortly after our first meeting but with a prayer for grace and forgiveness on his lips before passing away.

How many people have "heard" the sermons of the Good Samaritan or the Kingdom Inheritors of Matthew 25:34–36, yet do not take action? The hearing of the message does in fact stimulate faith, but faith without works (or action) is dead. This is the difference our Dad has made in our lives through his ministry and life; he taught us by example that it isn't enough to be "Hearers of the Word," but to make a difference in this world, we have to be "Doers." "Doers" are not stagnant, dormant, or unchanging. Doers are just the opposite, and thank God that we are constantly changing and growing because He knows we are still far from perfect!

This constant growth is another aspect that I've been privileged to observe and to learn from my Dad over the years. I'm so proud to have watched my Dad grow in grace and pray that I can grow more in grace like he has. His lessons in grace taught me through the Gospels and by example that there are definitely right and wrong choices everyday; we don't always make the right choice, but God's forgiveness has a boundless supply of grace to remove our honestly confessed sins as far from us as the east from the west. When we make a bad choice that leads us down the wrong path, God doesn't disinherit us, but He waits patiently for us to turn around (repent) and come back home to His open arms. I learned that people can do bad things and make bad choices. I learned that bad choices frequently have bad and lingering consequences; consequences that can remain to be dealt with even after God has forgiven the sinner. There is precisely the beauty of God's Grace; God's ability to see that we all are sinners and to love us anyway. He loves us so much that He searched us out, that He sold all His possessions to purchase us, and that He sent His Son as the ultimate sacrifice to redeem us.

Finally, my Dad's lessons in grace taught me there are only two types of people in the world, and God loves them both; those who have received the gift (redemption through Jesus) and those who have not received. Remember that while we were yet sinners, God loved us so much that He sacrificed His only Son? This lesson from my Dad and my heavenly Father taught me the difference between sin and the sinner; it helped me understand why His greatest commandment to us was to "Love one another." We are all God's creation, and what Creator would not long to see everyone of His creations redeemed? What better way to demonstrate His love to those who haven't yet received His Gift than by showing compassion and care for them?

As we go about trying to be "Doers," probably the most important thing I'm continuing to learn from my Dad and my heavenly Father is the simplicity of my role as a "Doer" versus God's role. I was taught that above all other commandments that I should love my neighbor as myself. I'm prone to making it complicated by trying to "do" what isn't mine to do, making judgments of people versus judging an action, worrying if I'm doing enough to meet others' expectations instead of just doing my best work today and sharing some compassion with someone who needs it, or just getting trapped in all the business of life and forgetting to show the love. I'm not trying to oversimplify the Great Commandment; if it were so simple to achieve, the world would be a much better place. What I am saying, however, is that when my life gets too hectic and complicated, it's almost always because I am over "doing" the wrong things and neglecting to honor God by not "doing" more of the "one thing."

Thanks Dad for raising us in a home where we could not only hear the Truth but also see the Truth demonstrated daily. Most importantly, thanks that you and Mom equipped us to go out and do the things you had taught us through sermons and life. Keep us in your prayers that we will continue to grow in our love for the Father and for others.

David

Let Brotherly Love Continue

Change had come into the life of Northside Christian Center, and God's change is always for the best. When God brings forth change, it is always to continue His will and purpose in the earth. Change will come to test us and see if we will move forward with the Holy Spirit or camp out in a comfortable and pleasant place where we can simply lay back and just flow downstream without responsibility or challenge. At Northside, we experienced an atmosphere of a richer and deeper love and relationship with the Lord and with the people we served. Of course, there will always be those who will complain and want to go back to a more familiar place where they can feel that everything is under their control, and some will go back and discontinue their walk in the Spirit. I believe Northside was ready for this change; they had circled this mountain until things had become dull and unproductive. They were ready to reach out to the community and to become involved with foreign missions as well as home missions. We believed the Lord was pleased with what the church was doing, so we moved along in ministering a message of grace and love and releasing faith in our hearts to reach out to see who we were in Christ and what our potential was as we preached His promises and embraced them with faith. We continued to witness the church filling up with new people, and this caused a fresh wave of hope to move over the people. Excitement is always the result when people are being blessed of God and people are giving their lives over to the Lord Jesus Christ. God's beautiful grace was surely unfolding before our very eyes, and we were the recipients who were being filled with His glory.

Lasting Results from Change

The change in ministry and activity within the structure of Northside was producing some very fruitful results. We seldom notice when growth is taking place until it has developed into a different stage of life, and then we stand back and say, "My, I can't believe that you have grown so fast." The natural eye is not designed to have the ability to see growth take place. It is like the seed dropped into the ground and hidden for a certain length of time, and all of a sudden, you look out one morning and green color covers the ground, and you get excited to see the results of change in the life of a seed. What you see coming up through the earth is a green blade, which is quite different from the dark brown small seed you planted seven days ago. That is change! That is a guarantee that life will continue in the earth.

Sometimes, it is difficult to share what the Lord is doing without being misunderstood of boasting of your own work. I refuse to let that happen in these writings because the title of this book should tell us what the whole theme speaks of, the unfolding of God's grace, and if it is of grace, it cannot be brought about by works! This book is about exalting God and His amazing, wonderful grace.

Between 1965 and 1979, many wonderful things took place in the church at Northside Assembly and its people. Two remarkable works of grace developed during these fourteen years of change and blessings. Oh yes, there were battles to fight, valleys to cross, mountains to climb, but if Jesus walks alongside you, He makes it possible for you to meet every trial and battle with hope and strength. We will not bore you with the battles, but I will say that we fought a good fight and lived to rejoice in the victory of it.

El Rancho Del Ray and Other Missions

Missions have always been a priority in ministry for Northside Christian Center, and the Lord has always had a unique way of introducing new missions to the church. In 1979, we were introduced to a beautiful family who were the founders and directors over a boys' ranch in Mexico. El Rancho Del Rey lay nestled between two beautiful mountain ranges overlooking the entire area of the Rancho. Hank and Anne Moller were led by the Holy Spirit to this location with a burning vision to start a home for boys who were homeless or whose homes could not properly support them. Since 1955, El Rancho Del Rey's home for boys has ministered to hundreds of homeless boys by caring for them in various ways. The boys receive an education; they are fed, clothed well, and always have the Gospel available to them, meeting regularly each week for service. The boys are led to a saving knowledge of the Lord Jesus; they are taught the scripture and participate in the services by giving a word of testimony, leading in prayer, and they are known for worshiping the Lord in music and song. Northside Christian Center has grown close to this mission over the years between 1979 until this very day.

Northside Christian Center has maintained a communication with around fifteen different missions, and our vision is to continue to add to the missions that the Lord brings into our reach. Embracing and supporting missions, home and foreign, is the key to the heart of Father God because God so loved the world that He gave His only begotten son that whosoever believeth upon Him will never perish but will have eternal life. Go ye therefore into all the world, and preach the Gospel to every creature; whosoever believeth and is baptized will be saved, he that believeth not shall be damned. God will bless and sustain a church that will be generous to those who are not able to help themselves.

God Does the Strangest Things

Our Father God must have humor, and His humor must be much greater than man's because He is greater than all others. There is no God before Him or shall there be any after Him. While praying on a Sunday evening here in the church, I heard this still small voice speak in my heart "Nicaragua," and it was accented with the Spanish accent so clearly. At first, I was startled because I was caught unaware by hearing the name of a country—a country that I hardly knew existed, and I didn't even know its location—but I knew that I must pursue the voice I heard.

As we began our evening service, I announced to the congregation that I would be going to the country of Nicaragua very soon. I never realized it, but I was going on a journey that would continue for years. This was a journey where the Lord directed me to work in a unique ministry of missions I never dreamed of. Why did I say that God had a sense of humor? Because at the age of seventy, after pastoring churches for fifty years, He calls me to leave pastoral work and go to the field and work. If it had been me doing the calling, I would not have sent an old man to the field, but God did. I will explain why: I owed him one. Well, really not one but all, but the humor in it was that He intended to collect this one in particular.

Let me explain. In the year of 1954, when the Lord called me into ministry, He spoke these words to me in the Spirit while I was praying: "Go ye out into the highways and hedges with your feet shod with the preparation of peace, and compel my people to come into my house that my house might be full." After that Word was spoken to me, I didn't go out into the highways and hedges. I went to the church house behind a pulpit for fifty years, not making any attempt to fulfill that first calling to mission. Sometimes you and I forget what the Lord says, but God does not forget, and that I knew quite well because fifty years later, while praying here in the church, the Spirit speaks again, clear and strong, and says, "Nicaragua." There could be no mistaking that now is the time to go!

My First Missionary Journey

Although I had visited a few missions before, this one was different; instead of someone else being responsible for the work, I found that I was carrying the ball. It was up to me to follow the direction of the Lord into the work that He had called me to. In the spring of 1999, two men here at Northside Christian Center and I purchased tickets to a city and country that I had never visited before. I had contacted the Scott Mauldin family that we were coming and that we would like to spend our time with them and observe their work there. This was very exciting but very strange; we could truly say with our Father Abraham that we were going, not knowing just where. We had set our visit for ten days, which was about five too many since we had no definite plans for our mission; regardless of how we valued the time, the Lord used it to acquaint us with the country and had us meeting people who would be of value to our work in the country in future visits.

Just less than one year prior to our arriving in the country of Nicaragua, in October 1998, Hurricane Mitch, the most powerful and destructive hurricane of the Atlantic hurricane season, had left a great part of Nicaragua devastated. Homes were washed away, people were swept away with the floods, and crops were wiped out, leaving much of the population of the country without homes or food. The family whom we were staying with drove to the edge of a village that they were working with. That day, we met under the shade of a huge mango tree near a little clinic, where around sixty people, leaders of their village, met to discuss with the family what could be done to help them survive the aftermath of Hurricane Mitch. I was given the opportunity to speak to the group that was meeting that day, and as I spoke to them and prayed for them, we discovered their greatest need at the time was corn seed to replant their crops so that they could have tortillas.

God is so good, and He is good all the time. At this particular time, it was easy to see because the men who came with me spoke up and said that they have brought extra money to give for needs that may arise; I had also brought more than I needed for myself and also mentioned that we could call back to the church and have extra money sent to purchase corn seed. Within a few minutes, we had enough money to buy enough seed to plant acres of corn.

At this point and time again, I heard that still small voice within my heart saying, "On this mission, you will help to plant corn, but from hereafter, you will plant churches." I thought that was a big order for such a small man, but God means what He says and never forgets a command. So please try to remember when the Lord speaks plainly to you that He won't forget what He says. Get ready to either obey His voice or live with the consequences because God's Word is not to be ignored nor will it return to Him empty and void. This was the highlight of my first trip into the highways and hedges that the Lord spoke to me in 1954.

God's Tests Are Always Productive

Even though I had not witnessed any major happenings on my first visit to Nicaragua, I came home excited about the potential of God's Word and what it could perform. "The next mission, you will not plant corn seed but churches." How, Lord? Living by faith is the most exciting way of life that man will ever discover. When you go out not knowing where you are going but you go by faith, you know you are in God's will and that He has something up His sleeve that He is not letting you in on at the present. This was my feeling as I returned home from my first encounter on the mission field.

On my second mission, Gene Ricks and Jack Wills accompanied me. This trip was a ringer; you have to know something about playing horseshoes to know what a ringer is. You are a winner when you make a ringer. This mission consisted of a taste of real missionary life. There was already a group of men and women in Nicaragua who make up the team that we were working with. This group consisted of a church family who were experts in medical work and also trained in going out into the village and witnessing to the villagers. They were just a great group of men and women who loved God and wanted to serve Him by ministering to the people.

We camped in a small village for two days and a night. This entailed sleeping out in the open; however, we had the covering of a gazebo over us. We threw our little mats down on the gazebo floor and lay down to try to get a little sleep. I think this would have worked fine, but the pigs wanted to run back and forth under the gazebo. We were not prodigals; nevertheless, we slept with the pigs that night, and the mosquitoes were not friendly either. The bathroom facilities were quite a distance from where we slept, so that presented quite a problem. Oh well, that's all in the life of the missionary, and looking back at the situation, I enjoyed it all.

The ringer that I mentioned earlier was that on this visit, we decided to plant a church just a mile or so from the place where we camped. In the little village of Popalon, we planted our first church, a beautiful little brick church, and on the day of dedication, the house was full of beautiful people, many children, and even people standing outside. It was the joy of my life because I had witnessed the first fruit of the Word that I received many years ago. We named this church My Father's House, after the Word of the Lord.

Even though we felt victory and joy over planting our first church in the country of Nicaragua, the ending of this joy was very short-lived. The church was built in a remote area where the people were very poor, and many of the people had to move away from Popalon to find work to survive. There was no shepherd to care for the flock of Popalon. This seemed to be a discouraging factor concerning our church-planting mission, but the Word of the Lord was sure. There was no thought of giving up, quitting, or turning back; we had begun the journey and intended to walk it out to the finish line and would not look back.

By this time, I had reached over my threescore and ten years, and many people seemed to think that I was a bit old to take up a mission that required so much effort and work. I was more excited and happier to know that I had the potential of reaching many people by preparing a place for them to come together and worship the Lord than I had ever been in my fifty years of ministry.

Third Time Victory Comes

You know that there is something special about the number 3. Oh, well, I know that there are many who have no confidence in numbers, but the Bible is full of them. In almost all of them, the number 3 has a message of victory. How about this one: "Destroy this temple and in three days I will raise it up," speaking of His body and the resurrection of Jesus Christ.

Well, there was something special about our third visit into the country of Nicaragua. My friend and brother in Christ, Gene Ricks, called me one Sunday evening and said, "I had a missionary preaching for me this morning, and guess where he is from?" Of course, I said, "Nicaragua," and Gene asked me if we could have him that Sunday evening for service. I said, "Send him on up." That night, Brother Fred Womack, his wife, and his daughter were with us and preached for us.

Our church loved the Womack family at first sight, and we began working together in the Lord for over the next ten years. A mission trip had already been planned, so we were invited to visit the Womack family when we came down. Gene and I had planned on spending two weeks on this mission. We spent the first week with the Scott Mauldin family and the second week with the Fred Womack family. This trip carried us to Popalon, where the church was being built. Scott had gotten delayed on building because of the weather, so in order for us to dedicate the church while we were there, the workers had to speed up their work. While Scott was finishing with the Popalon church building, Gene and I went to visit Fred Womack, who lived in the city of Esteli some ninety miles north of Managua.

When we arrived at Esteli, Brother Fred had already scheduled every day of our visit to travel to some of the existing churches to get acquainted with their pastors and people. He had already prepared our schedule because he shared the same vision as we, to plant churches in Nicaragua. I will never forget that schedule; he had it written and taped to the wall. The schedule was written in large letters so that it would be easy to read. He thoroughly went through the list of churches and city names with us knowing it would be a bit difficult for us to remember and pronounce the words in Spanish, but to my surprise, I remember the names of the churches and their locations until this very day. I can pronounce them, and each one of them still sticks to my mind. My heart was reaching out to the people and the work that needed to be done for the people to know the Lord and serve Him better.

To many of our readers, the names of places will mean very little to you, but some of you will know them and have been there with us. The very first city that we visited was the city of Occotal. We arrived there around lunchtime, found our pastor, ate lunch, and proceeded to the church.

When I saw the church, I was grieved in my spirit because it was a little poorly built wood building wherein you could see through the cracks in the walls. In my mind, I could see a nice masonry building standing here filled with people praising and worshiping the Lord, and I praise the Lord since that kind of building stands there today! The same little humble pastor and family still minister there. We give thanks first to our Lord Jesus, who supplied the funds for the materials, and for all our friends who reached out to us and shared their love through their giving. This building came later after the first visit, but it came.

Also in the city of Occotal, Nicaragua Church Planting built another church; we call it the church on the mountain because the people had to move the top of the mountain in order to construct the building. Then Nicaragua Church Planting bought an existing building, so now in the city of Occotal, there stands three places of worship that came out of the call to highways and hedges where people meet regularly to worship the Lord. As I write, I am reminded of the Lord's message to Zerubbabel while the temple in Jerusalem was being restored: "This is the word of the Lord to Zerubbabel: Not by might nor by power, but by my Spirit, Says the Lord." When translated, this prophetic word means that when men work within their own strength and power, they can take credit for the work they do, but when the Spirit of the Lord performs the work through its ability, the Lord gets all the glory from the project. Men struggle; the Holy Spirit flows!

The Desert Shall Blossom as a Rose

Many times, I had stood behind the pulpit at Northside Christian Center and spoke prophetically these very words, and when they were spoken, I was always filled with awe for wondering just how and when this would ever happen. The words of prophesy that would come forth were like this: "My word and spirit will flow like a river from this place into dry and desolate and barren places. Rivers will break out and water the dry and thirsty land and bring forth life." Of course, these things were taking place in various places, but I had not witnessed them from the ministry here at NCC. As we began to go into the poverty-stricken places in the country of Nicaragua, I began to preach the Gospel to the poor, and seeing people come alive in Christ reminded me of the words we had heard in our services back home.

Give Me That Mountain

One of my favorite scriptures is found in Joshua 14:12, after Israel had crossed the Jordan River and moved into their inheritance. Caleb addressed Joshua and said the following:

> You remember what Moses said 40 years ago that the mountain of Hebron would be mine when we took the land, as my strength was then so it is now, I am as strong now as on the day that Moses sent me, so give me this mountain!

As we stood with our mission group just outside the town of Jalapa in the far north part of Nicaragua, I looked up toward a green-covered hill that we were to be given to plant a church, and as I looked at this beautiful location, I said aloud, "Give me this mountain." As it were, the city of Jalapa deeded that piece of property over to the church, and today, there stands a beautiful church building that houses a congregation of people who love the Lord and a pastor who loves the Lord and His people. This is only one of many churches that we have been able to plant through the help of the Lord and His people, and of course, we give much honor to the missionaries who committed their lives and work in order to spearhead this work in the country of Nicaragua.

I pay honor and tribute to the Fred and Lavanda Womack family today for the great work they accomplished there. Had it not been for them, Nicaragua Church Planting could have never gone forward with its ministry.

God's Grace Continues to Unfold in Nicaragua

As we continued to go in and out of the country of Nicaragua, it began to feel like my second home, or my home away from home. This was not easily understood because the language was difficult, the food was not always what we liked, and actually, nothing was convenient, yet I loved every minute that I spent in the country. Some of the roads that we traveled were very rough and some even a bit dangerous. Sometimes it would take us hours to travel a few miles, but somehow, this didn't seem to be a problem, for as we traveled, we laughed and rejoiced concerning the work that was being done there in the country.

I would sit with the people in their church services, not understanding a word that was being spoken, yet I felt comfortable and at home. If such a thing were possible, I would consider myself a part of this country and bonded to it by the love for the country and its people. This gives me some understanding why God has favored us in unfolding His wonderful grace by supplying the funds for all the buildings and keeping us from becoming sick while in the country.

Our missionary would often say to me, "You don't ever get sick like most people who come down." I knew the difference, but I feared and respected the Lord too much to reply to those kinds of words because I always knew it was Jesus who kept me well and feeling good while I was in the country. I would always come home filled with joy and praise for what the Lord did while we were there. I did not dare to even sound like I was boasting of myself because I knew quite well the Lord had His hand on me, keeping me well while doing His will.

The only time I got sick was when I was disobedient to the advice the missionary gave me. Brother Fred had warned me time and again, "Brother Billy, the people cook with cooking oil here that you are not adjusted to, and it will cause you to be sick if you eat it." Well, Eve ate the fruit and died; I ate the cooking oil and almost died.

We were coming from San Carlos to Granada on a boat one night. The time was about midnight when I smelled the fragrance of fish being fried. I slipped off down into the snack bar where the fish were being cooked and never inquired as to what kind of oil they were using. I ordered a couple of fish and enjoyed them immensely. I paid a high price for that meal because in about an hour, I was giving them back to the fish as I hung over the side of the boat rail. The picture would have won a prize if someone had taken it right then because Brother Fred reached out and took my suspenders and pulled back on them to keep me from falling overboard. I am sure when he thinks of that incident, it causes him to chuckle and probably think, *I told him not to eat anything cooked with that oil, but he didn't listen.*

When we disobey someone who has been there and done that, it will cost us plenty. I have stayed far away from food that has been cooked in that type of oil ever since that night that I fed the fish at midnight.

When God Manifests His Glory

When I recall the miracles that accompanied Nicaragua Church Planting, I marvel at the wisdom of my God. You must understand that I had no regular way to finance the buildings that were built, and yet this was what I was called upon to do. Well, I thought, I have to start somewhere. I began by sending out a newsletter called *Nicaragua Church Planting*, and along with that, I began to tell my friends and churches about my new adventure of planting churches in the country of Nicaragua.

To my surprise, when I took the first short step, God took a giant step. I had recently posted in the newsletter that we had found a piece of property that we wanted to convert over into a church. It was a large thatched-roof gazebo-type building that had a brick wall about four feet high surrounding it. The entire property would cost us three thousand dollars. As soon as the newsletter had time to reach the hand of the caller, I received a call saying, "I want to purchase that property you mentioned in the newsletter." I hesitated for a moment and said, "Do you understand how much the property cost?" His answer to that was, "You will have a check in the mail tomorrow for the land and building." I thanked him and hung up the phone, thinking, *I can't believe this!* Our first church already paid for, and that has been around twenty-five churches ago, and the Lord has always come through for all of them.

I want our readers to understand; if we will hear His voice and harden not our hearts but obey the still small voice, we will see the glory of our God. I have a dear brother in Christ that has a saying: "If it is God's will, it is God's bill," and God is never late on His payments. He is right on time; praise the Lord!

In the events of Nicaragua Church Planting, there are many miracles and works of the Lord that we can share with you. Our cup runs over as I meditate on the many times the Lord reached out His hand in order to supply a need, to keep us from danger, to open up a new location for a church, and to give us many, many Holy Spirit–anointed services where people were saved, filled, and healed.

Miracles Happen Unannounced

In the little village town of Limay, Nicaragua, a group had formed together in Bible study and prayer meeting. They had formed a nucleus of people large enough to qualify them for a church building. I had shared with our church about this property for a church building, and on a Sunday evening, before service began, I was stopped in the aisle by some of the faithful members of NCC. They said to me, "We want to buy the property at Limay for the church." Again, the Lord had moved the hearts of His people to share in planting churches in the country of Nicaragua.

Our very next mission trip carried us to the town of Limay, where we had purchased the lot for the church building. That afternoon, the group that had gone with me and the people of the village of Limay gathered on the lot to dedicate it to the work of the Lord. We joined hands and began to pray for the property and for the people of the village of Limay. After we had finished our prayer and greeted everyone, we walked on up to the house that joined the church lot for the evening service. Little did any of us know that we were about to witness a wonderful miracle of healing that evening.

At the end of the service, our missionary stood and announced that one of the men who came down from Texas, Richard Simmison, told us that his daughter had a dream that while we were in the country of Nicaragua, we would see a miracle of the healing of a young child. Richard, for some reason, had forgotten to remind us of that dream in the service. When our missionary announced this, the lady of the house stood and said, "That's my son." When we asked her where he was, she replied, "He is in the back room of the house." We asked her to bring him out so that we could pray for him, so she went back and brought him into the service. As usual, we laid our hands on him and prayed and ask the Lord to heal him.

There was not a great emotional feeling after the prayer of just a simple prayer; however, after we prayed for the boy, he went outside and began playing with the other kids who were there. We thought that was a bit unusual. The service ended, and everyone said their good-byes and dispersed and went home. The rest of the story did not come until Monday of the following week. The missionaries and I were traveling to another church for a meeting, and our route took us through Limay. We decided to stop by the house where we had prayed for the little boy, and as soon as we stopped the car, the mother came running out, shouting, "My son is healed, my son is healed!" We all were so happy and thankful that her son had been healed. When we asked her what his sickness consisted of, she said, "Mountain leprosy." Wow, leprosy! Had we known he had leprosy, we may have been a bit reluctant to have even laid our hands on him. We had seen the Lord Jesus do a miracle of healing, and we rejoiced and gave thanks.

Pajarito (The Little Bird)

In the life of church-planting ministry, Pajarito stands out far above many of our experiences of planting churches. Pajarito is located on a very fertile plateau where the people grow several kinds of grain and vegetables, and also cattle are raised for their living. There are so many interesting things involved with our mission work that time and space will not allow us to tell it all.

For starters, go with me one day to the little village of Pajarito. Our missionaries were well aware of the heavy rains that had just come and washed rocks into the narrow road that we were to take going up to the village. But to their surprise, when we reached the entrance to the road that would carry us into the village, someone had gone before us with a bulldozer and cleared all the rock from the road. We found no blockages as we entered the village. Many of the people of Pajarito were very dedicated to the Lord and to the church that they were attending eight or ten miles away. Of course, not many people here in the States would understand people walking for miles to attend church, but hunger, thirst, and commitment to Christ determine what people will do to serve Him.

Each Sunday, the people who lived here at Pajarito walked to the town of Achuapa to attend their church services. I was thinking ten miles to church and ten miles back home after church will consume a full day; these people deserve a church of their own here in their village.

Not only were the people committed to spend their full Sundays going to church, but also they were found to be committed in working toward building their own church. This is awesome! Their lot where the church would be planted was covered with beautiful trees, and of course, in

Nicaragua, you are not allowed by law to cut a tree. The people had to pay to cut their trees so the lot would be prepared to build the church. As our custom was before we planted a church, we would have a dedication service to dedicate the property to the Lord and to His work. Even today, I still feel the excitement rise within me as the missionaries made the dedication for the property and drove a stake into the ground, making our claim to dedicate this lot, and the work will be given to the glory of God.

Soon the men of the village began to build the church with their strength and knowledge. First, having no lumber for their foundation, wall studs, and rafters, they cut all of this material out with chain saws; all their framework was cut out with chain saws. Some distance from the church, the men made their own brick, built their kilns, cooked the brick, and used them in bricking the outside of the building. Nicaragua Church Planting came in and purchased the roof for them, and at this time, there stands a beautiful building, where people gather to worship the Lord without walking ten miles to the church in Achuapa.

On one of our visits to Nicaragua, we scheduled Pajarito Church as one of our projects to see how the church was doing, and to encourage the pastor and his people. Pastor Gene Ricks was with me on this visit as he had been part of previous missions into Nicaragua. It was three weeks after I had a knee implant, so my walking was very limited. When we reached the road that led us up to the church of Pajarito, they had saddled a mule for me to ride. The road was very muddy and slick, and a light rain was still falling, so it made walking very difficult. Well, I mounted the mule with some help as someone took hold of my right leg and lifted it up over the back of the mule, so we were off to Pajarito.

What a ride, Terry! We made the ride up and back, but I suppose the aftermath of the ride was my worse punishment because the picture of me riding the mule was sent to the local newspaper here. When certain people saw it and knew I had just recently had a knee implant, some panicked, especially my therapist, who saw me for my next treatment and informed me that of all things, I didn't need to be riding horses until the knee had completely healed. Six years have come and gone, and yet I hold some blessed and fond memories of the church and the village of Parjarito, Nicaragua.

New Doors Began to Open

In 2009, Nicaragua Church Planting began to experience a transition, and a concern for the ministry of planting churches was felt among those who were part of our mission team. We had not seen a change in building churches in the ten years that we had worked in the country of Nicaragua. The change consisted of several different things that came up in the fellowship that we were working with. Our missionary for the fellowship in Nicaragua became ill and had to come out into the States because of health issues. The fellowship only had one missionary to place over Nicaragua, who was already covering four countries, and this was a little too much for him to be able to give us the time we needed to plant a church when we were ready. Each church that we ever planted was built as soon as our finances were available, and our brother was not able to stop what he was doing and spend time with us to build, so change was inevitable.

God's grace already had a great plan laid out for Nicaragua Church Planting, and a plan that would open doors that we never dreamed of. God had given us great success prior to this change because Nicaragua Church Planting had already been involved in building at least twenty churches for the fellowship, so we gave the Lord praise for these churches that were built and for the precious people and pastors who made up the churches.

After leaving the fellowship we were working with, we were invited to Nicaragua by another missionary who was a bishop, a director of over 660 churches in the country of Nicaragua. Our brother opened his arms and received us as if he had known us for life. We began in 2010 by building our first church for the Church of God of Cleveland, Tennessee, in the small town of Tisma. This church was built during the rainy season of the year, so you would think we would have to pick our time to work, but that was not the case here. On this project, eight of our missionary team members came down to build. We had a great team of men, and their heart was set on building and seeing the church finished. Time in building was shortened because two of our team members suggested that we rent a concrete mixer to help speed up the work, and it did. Most of our buildings were built with masonry blocks sealed with cement, which was made by mixing up the cement on the ground.

Again, we witnessed a miracle while building the church at Tisma. Each morning when we left our motel rooms in Managua, the clouds would be very heavy and rainy. We were riding out to work in a pickup, so two people had to ride in the back. They would protect themselves the best they could by wearing raincoats, but that alone did not keep them dry. Each day, we would drive in the rain until we were a mile or so from the building location, and then the rain would stop, and when we reached the location, it would be dry.

The first day or so, we never paid it much attention, but when it continued to rain every day until we would come near our building and the rain would stop, we all agreed the Lord was controlling the rain so that we could continue our work on the church. We all called it a miracle! Dedication for the Tisma church took place a few months later when Bobby Crow and I went down to make the dedication. This was a beautiful event, many bright colors were displayed, and the house was filled with people and people standing on the outside. Joy filled our hearts as we cut the ribbon and walked inside, with the pastor and the people following us.

Full Circle, Back to Our Father's House

While building the Tisma church, another church was already in the plans. God's timing is always perfect, and His plans are always designed to exalt His Son and to bless His people. Our missionary pastor lived in the village of Granadilla, near the city of Granada. He had already secured the land to build in Grandilla, and our mission team had agreed this was the place for our next church plant. Granadilla is a village where 190 families live. It is a beautiful part of the country with all its greenery and fruit, and is elevated above the surrounding area on a plateau of rich and fertile ground.

In the year of 2011, our mission team flew down for a two-week visit to work on the church of Granadilla. This visit was filled with excitement and joyful fellowship. Our team made friends quickly with the nationals who were building the temple. Each day, all our team went for lunch at our missionary's home, where we always found a long table filled with all kinds of good things to eat. Our time at lunch was filled with laughter and rich fellowship as we broke bread together. Our men had grown so close to the men who were working on the building that they wanted to buy each worker a pair of work shoes. The last day of our visit we had somewhat of a celebration where the shoes were handed out to the men, and it seemed like God's love came and bonded all of us together.

When the church was completed, it was named My Father's House. Only this time, it was not like our experience at Popalon; this time, the people filled the house and continued until this day to gather and lift their voice in high praise to our Lord Jesus Christ. In October 2011, we returned to Granadilla to dedicate My Father's House, where we were met by hundreds of people who came to join in the celebration of their new church. After My Father's House, there was Laural Galan, Palmira, Quisala, and Christo Rey.

An Open Door That No Man Can Shut

Thank God that He mandates for us some of His plans and purposes for ministry. In 1979, the Lord began to summon NCC with a mandate to rise up and build once again. From time to time, the Holy Spirit would imply that it is time to build a larger facility. The existing sanctuary was not sufficient for what the Lord was about to do, so as time progressed, we were in limbo waiting to hear more clearly His will for building.

What the church was waiting for suddenly happened! One weekend in September of 1979, I was attending a convention in Okmulgee, Oklahoma. In one of the morning services, a prophet walked over to me, laid his hand on me, and began to prophesy the Word of the Lord: "Ye saith the Lord, you will be forced to rise up and build larger." Of course this was a confirmation to what the church had been hearing for some time. I had to drive back to Carthage for our weekend services because we were having a man and his wife in to minister for us on Sunday.

As our brother and his wife were ministering in music and preaching, the lady stepped off the platform, walked over to me, laid her hands on me, and began to give me the Word of the Lord: "You will be forced to rise up and build larger." Same word came from two completely different people who didn't even know each other. All the church heard the word of prophesy given and was convinced that the time was ripe to build.

From this time until the facility was completed, a continual flow of God's grace was manifested to all who had any part of the ministry of NCC. When we received our first building-fund offering, it amounted to sixty-two thousand dollars. When the amount was announced, some said, "He meant 6,200." Some were stunned with surprise, but some said, "That's God and His grace." With our building fund and a hundred-thousand-dollar loan, the building began and never slowed down until it was completely finished. Everything was finished except the parking lot, and one of our faithful and committed members, who ran a construction company, put down the parking lot and never charged the church for their labor. Until this day, I feel indebted to this brother; however, he has already gone on home to be with the Lord. At this juncture, there are many people for whom we will always be grateful for their generosity and love, especially to the Walter Hudson family who was responsible for building the church.

Northside Christian Center was dedicated to the Lord and to His glory on Easter 1980. The church was blessed with many people who came for this special occasion.

The head carpenter and some of his men were there. The Kendells, who gave the Word of the Lord for the people to "rise up and build," were present with their ministry, and many others came to help celebrate the dedication and opening of a new church. It was a day filled with joy and thanksgiving.

The threefold vision that had previously been mentioned began to be ministered from the pulpit and discussed among the people. This vision was made up in three stages: evangelism, enlargement, and education. At this time, the church began to see this vision materialize. The church was reaching out to new people with a message of love and fellowship in Christ, and the pews began filling up more and more each Sunday morning. In 1985, the Lord presented me with a mandate for the third stage of the vision: a mandate to enter into a Christian education project. At this point, I had no other options; it was to initiate Christian education, or the book was closed to me. I chose the inevitable; I was not ready to go to the house yet.

Northside Christian Center had members who were ablaze with the vision of Christian education, and with that unction, we began to purchase the materials for the new building to house the students and staff. This was one of the greatest challenges that we had ever encountered at this point of ministry. Even though the church was financially able to build and comply with the requirements of starting the program, we had people telling us, "You can't have a school," "You can't offer the students the proper subjects that public school offers them," "You don't have qualified teachers," and "Why don't you just give it up and concede the church just can't comply with offering the students what they need to enter college and higher-education studies when they graduate from high school?"

At that time, we were pastoring the ex-superintendent and his wife, along with ten other public school teachers, and none of them could agree with the vision of a small church maintaining an educational system. To this entire negative attitude, my reply was, "That is not what I heard the Lord say," and continued getting started by the fall semester. By the grace of the Lord, we began with about twenty-seven students and four or five teachers. The education project started like most projects start: with a bang. We were off with things going pretty well the first year. Since we were unprepared for the task, we allowed some problems to slip through the doors, and division took its toll on not only the school but also on the church members who had their students attending the school.

I, as pastor over the church and school, felt a bit helpless and hopeless, not knowing just how to handle the situation, but God and His grace were sufficient and came running to our rescue. We took a loss in finance and in people, but by the grace of our Lord, we survived. Today, we give thanks to our Lord for unfolding His marvelous grace before us, like a red carpet being unfolded before us, and that still small voice within saying, "Son, keep on walking." It is so true that when the strength of man runs out that the Lord is there to reach down, pick you up, dust you off, and set you on the road of His will once again. We have lived to see and enjoy this threefold vision come into operation. The vision is not totally complete today, but it is increasing year by year with an increase of students and a well-qualified teaching staff and principal.

The vision is also reaching our community little by little and is one of the most fruitful ministries in the area. Our testimony is, "When God is responsible for a birth, He will continue to be responsible for sustaining that birth." God will never bring anything to birth then walk away and leave it to perish. He not only has the power to give life but also has the power to see that life nourish and grow.

Today, twenty-eight years later, Northside Christian Academy has an administration staff of four and a staff of seven teachers who are well-trained and qualified to give our students an education that will teach them not only how to make a living but also how to live in this dark world and bring forth the light of life.

Thirteen Years with Our Baptist Friends

God is always coming up with surprises—some pleasant, some not so pleasant. But these last thirteen years, the Lord led us to one of the most rewarding areas of our life. You might say He poured out a double portion of His blessings upon our lives. One Sunday morning, as I sat relaxed and ready to be blessed by the ministry of Northside Christian Center, the Holy Spirit began to tug at my heart concerning a little missionary Baptist Church near Deadwood, Texas. I really tried to listen to the message that our pastor was sharing with us, but somehow, there was a stronger and more definite Word coming that no matter how I tried to turn off wouldn't go away. What I was hearing in the Holy Spirit was, "There is a little flock of my people at Panola Baptist that has no one to feed them and to love them, and I am calling you to go."

I was familiar with this voice, so after service that morning, I went straight home, called one of the members of Panola Baptist, and let them know that I was available to come and minister if they wanted me to come. The lady whom I was talking to said that she would ask the members that afternoon and call me back that evening. What was so surprising about this event was that fifty years ago, I was a member of a missionary Baptist Church, and after I had received the Holy Spirit baptism, I never felt comfortable staying with the church because I knew I would create problems for the pastor. I stepped aside thinking I would never be a member of a Baptist Church again, but God changed that! The Lord was teaching me a lesson that I will always be grateful for, one that has made me comfortable with the Lord's people regardless of what church they attend.

That same Sunday evening, the lady from Panola Baptist called me and said, "Brother Billy, they will be happy for you to come and minister." This was one of those pleasant surprises that God chose to bless me with, and for it I will be grateful. God's marvelous grace continues to unfold right before my eyes so that I might learn what God is like.

In those thirteen years that we served at Panola Baptist, we witnessed God's goodness and grace as He formed things in place, both in the Spirit and in the natural. Carnal eyes would have never been able to behold some of the work of the Holy Spirit. For instance, one Sunday morning, in our service, we were led by the Spirit to challenge ourselves to a task that needed to be accomplished for years. The members at Panola Baptist wanted a place for fellowship and for special occasions for the community. As we discussed the matter, someone said, "Let's build it," and all eight of us said, "Let's do it!" We had about eight or ten attending members at that time and eleven thousand dollars in our church fund, which, if we were only depending on what we were seeing, there would have been no way, but there was God!

We began the construction with what we had, and God made up for the rest because He began to send us men from the community and men from Carthage to help us build. We were blessed with several members from Northside Christian Center and their pastor. One precious brother who lived over near Price, Texas, drove the distance each Saturday that we worked; he helped to build and wired the entire facility without receiving any compensation and purchased much of the electrical parts. Another brother in Christ came from Shreveport and helped faithfully in the building. Texas Baptist Builders were such a blessing as they came and framed and put the dry wall up while another brother painted the inside. Time will not permit us to mention all of those who helped and those who gave love offerings to purchase the materials. Last but by no means the least, the ladies from the church had the table spread with delicious food each Saturday that we worked, and this gave us a special time to fellowship with each other during the noon meal.

We share all these good things that occurred around building the fellowship hall to assure each of us that if we take one small step by faith, God will take the giant step to compensate all our needs. "But my God will supply all your need according to His riches in glory by Christ Jesus" (Philippians 4:19, KJV).

East of the River Pastors' Fellowship

Brother Jack Wills, who copastored with me most of the time that I served at Panola Baptist, shared equally in all the happenings at Panola Baptist. He labored not only throughout the building of the Fellowship Hall but also in preaching and teaching the Word of God. One day, he and I were discussing and praying about the ministry and what we could do to enlarge the community fellowship. We decided to begin what is called East of the River Pastors' Fellowship. We started by announcing a prayer breakfast at Panola Baptist and inviting six of the pastors whom we knew in the community, and at the said time, they all responded. There was joy knowing that ministry of different denominations could come together and enjoy the fellowship as we broke bread, prayed, and had a devotion from the Word of God. That was seven years ago, and the fellowship seems to be growing stronger each month that we meet.

In the early part of 2013, our time at Panola Baptist was finished, so we resigned, with both pastor and congregation agreeing that it was the Lord's will for us to resign from the church. We finished well with perfect unity with the people there and returned back to our church home at Northside Christian Center.

Maybe I haven't been serving as a church member long enough yet to prove what I have said for a long time, and our readers may not agree with this statement, especially preachers, but I have never thought that a God-called preacher could make a good church member. I am trying my best to prove myself wrong, but time will tell. Of course, I might need some confirmation to go along with my evaluation.

I value the ministry of preaching and teaching God's Word to be the highest priority of my life. From my perspective now, here is what I can conclude: I am now eighty-four years old and have served the Lord from the church for sixty of those years, and I am just as excited about what I believe God is doing and what He will continue to do throughout age without end. I have a great church home that covers the missions I still am involved in and a great pastor who is anointed to preach God's Word and to care for the people as a shepherd cares for his sheep. My heart is fixed and set on continuing to plant churches in the country of Nicaragua until God calls me home or tells me my work is finished in that country, but until that time occurs, I shall live to see the glorious, marvelous grace of God continue to unfold until I see His face.